INSURANCE AND INVESTING

[Insurance
Investing]

MONEYLIFE™ BASICS SERIES

ISBN 978-1-56427-253-9

Special thanks to George M. Hiller, JD, LLM, MBA, CFP® and Steven D. Humphrey, CFP® of the George M. Hiller Companies, LLC, Atlanta, Georgia for their professional contributions to this book.

For inquiries in Canada, please contact CrownCanada.ca or call 1-866-401-0626.

June 2008 Edition

CONTENTS

INTRODUCTION

This book will help you regardless of your stage of life. From teens needing car insurance to retirees needing to learn more about investment options—and everyone in between—you will find information to help you weigh important options.

Some people believe that having insurance or investments indicates a lack of trust in God. For them, it may. Some people also believe that seeking medical treatment indicates a lack of trust in God, and for them, it may. Although we do not judge them for their convictions, we do not share them.

At the same time, we recognize the constant temptation to put our trust in human devices rather than in God, and such trust is clearly misplaced. It's the "rather than" that creates the problem; it implies an "either-or" condition: Either we trust God to do something or we do it.

We believe this condition is unnecessary and that God expects us to take a "both-and" approach in our management of His resources: We both trust God to do something and we do it.

Consider these examples.

- Many Scriptures indicate that God will provide our needs, which Jesus emphasized in His sermon on the mount, particularly Matthew 6:25–7:12. But He also mandated that we work. God provides AND we work.
- He invites us to seek His wisdom, but He expects us to use the intelligence He gave us in making decisions. God gives wisdom AND we use our brains.
- He distributed money to three different men in the parable of the talents (Matthew

25:14-28), but He expected them, as His stewards, to do something with it—to put it to work for an increase. God entrusts resources AND we manage them for growth.

- He cares for the poor and needy, but He expects us to participate in meeting their needs (Matthew 25:31-46). God gives AND we give.

God has not called us to passivity. Trusting Him does not mean lack of action on our part. James drives this point in his second chapter. Using Abraham as an example, he says, *"...His faith and his actions were working together, and his faith was made complete by what he did"* (James 2:22, NIV).

How does this relate to insurance and investing? We should take responsibility to manage God's resources prudently while we trust Him implicitly for everything beyond our control. We act within the scope of what He has entrusted to us using the tools available to us.

We believe that insurance and investments are prudent management tools within the Master's expectation for our stewardship. We are also careful to keep them from eroding our complete dependence upon God, who alone is worthy of our trust. We look to Him for guidance, we act accordingly, and we trust Him for the results.

Help and Hope Are Here.

HELP HOPE

Crown exists to provide help, hope, and insight. These Help and Hope buttons appear whenever special information is available to assist and encourage you.

Please notice a few helpful features we include in every *MoneyLife™ Basics Series* book.

1. Appendix 1 is an introduction to Christ. If you (or someone you know) are uncertain about where you stand with God, this short introduction will guide you into an intimate relationship with Him.
2. Appendix 2, "God's Ownership & Financial Faithfulness," briefly explores a fundamental concept—one that frames the correct perspective on every financial principle in Scripture. If you don't understand this, you are likely to manage your resources with worldly wisdom. The world's approach to money management isn't always evil, but it is short-sighted (ignoring eternity), incomplete (ignoring the Creator/Controller/Provider), and usually in pursuit of the wrong goals.
3. Because we are committed to transformation rather than mere information, each chapter ends with a two-part exercise:
    - An Action Step you create based on your response to the chapter
    - A Celebration Plan for every Action Step completed

Please take advantage of these to maximize your experience in this small book. James 1:22 sums it up when it says, *"Do not merely listen to the word, and so deceive yourselves. Do what it says"* (NIV).

CHAPTER 1

INSURANCE

What Is Insurance?

In simple terms, insurance lets us pay a little now to cover future major expenses due to illness, death, accident, disaster, or theft.

Buying insurance is like storing grain for the winter months (Proverbs 6:6-8). Protecting ourselves against the cost of a catastrophic illness, which can devastate a family's finances, is a wise investment.

Unfortunately, insurance has become a means to "protect" against every possible contingency no matter how unlikely. This misuse of insurance can lead to greed, laziness, waste, and fear. But, worse than that, it can lead to dependence on insurance instead of on God, our ultimate provider.

Current Attitudes

Americans have developed an "insurance ethic" that often justifies cheating insurance companies. Some of the rationalizations include:

- Viewing the insurance company as impersonal. They don't really know anyone there, so it's not like they're cheating a real person. But an insurance company is comprised of employees, members/stockholders, policy holders, etc. When the company is cheated, all of these people suffer. As followers of Christ, we can live above this temptation by observing His command in Matthew 7:12: *"In everything, therefore, treat people the same way you want them to treat you."*

- Viewing the insurance company as wealthy. Many people believe the wealthy acquired their money dishonestly, making them fair game. Jesus enables us to overcome this judgmental attitude: *"Why do you look at the speck that is in your brother's eye, but do not notice the log that is in your own eye?...First take the log out of your own eye, and then you will see clearly to take the speck out of your brother's eye"* (Matthew 7:3, 5).

- Expecting too much from insurance—protection from any and every loss. No product can do this. Although God could protect us from every loss, He will not. To do so would not be in our best interest. Rather, He lovingly filters everything that occurs to us, guaranteeing that *"God causes all things to work together for good to those who love God, to those who are called according to His purpose"* (Romans 8:28).

- Desperation, brought on by fear. This may result from an emphasis on protecting rather than providing for the family. An obsession to protect every possession is a failure to recognize God's ownership—or at least a failure to internalize the comfort and peace His ownership offers. It is one thing to use insurance as a prudent steward; it is quite another to overburden our family's spending plan with inordinate insurance costs in an effort to protect our stuff. Throughout the Gospels, Jesus repeatedly encourages us not to fear or worry, assuring us that *"…your Father knows what you need before you ask him"* (Matthew 6:8).

Regardless of current attitudes, dishonesty is a violation of God's character. We must never rationalize it. God is ready to provide and bless your efforts in wonderful ways as you trust Him and demonstrate it by honestly doing the right things.

Biblical Perspective

If we understood and accepted our various responsibilities, there would be little need for insurance. When a family is in need, other families should respond. *"At this present time your abundance being a supply for their need, so that their abundance also may become a supply for your need, that there may be equality; as it is written, 'He who gathered much did not have too much, and he who gathered little had no lack'"* (2 Corinthians 8:14-15). Unfortunately, most are not at this point.

Insurance is most important in those situations in which a potential loss would be great. This is especially true when another's loss must be considered, as in automobile liability coverage. *"A prudent man sees evil and hides himself, the naive proceed and pay the penalty"* (Proverbs 27:12).

Choosing an Agent

Since your insurance agent will provide important counsel beyond your area of expertise, choose carefully.

1. As a first level of screening, ask the agent for references. Second, check the agent's level of experience. Don't deal with a nonprofessional agent or one who sells insurance part time. Also check to see if the agent has earned a professional designation, such as CLU (Chartered Life Underwriter), ChFC (Chartered Financial Consultant), CFP® (Certified Financial Planner), CPCU (Chartered Property and Casualty Underwriter), or RHU (Registered Health Underwriter). These designations won't guarantee that a particular agent is best for you but, at the very least, they do show that the agent has completed a disciplined course of study.

2. Expect cooperation. Be sure your agent thoroughly analyzes your insurance needs. Don't tolerate an agent who tries to pressure you into buying more insurance than you can afford or need.

3. Proverbs 1:5 says that *"a man of understanding will acquire wise counsel."* When it comes to insurance, the source of wisest counsel should be a knowledgeable, experienced Christian agent.

The average novice in the area of insurance will need the very best counsel possible. Thoroughly read everything the company asks you to sign. If you don't understand it, require the agent or company to write it out in language you can understand.

Also be sure you understand your policy before you buy it. Find out how much coverage it provides and if it has any exclusions. Don't wait until you file a claim to find out what your policy covers.

Choosing an Insurance Company

One of the most important insurance decisions you must make is choosing an insurance company. After all, the timely payment of your benefits depends on that company's stability. Although there are many good insurance companies not listed in the "top 20," dealing with a company in the top 20 usually is best for the inexperienced person.

As you go through this process of choosing an insurance agent and company, pray as God's steward for His wisdom and direction.

Section 1

PROPERTY AND CASUALTY INSURANCE

Home Owner's Insurance

A *home owner's insurance* policy covers calamities that could happen to your home and its contents. It also covers liability from many things—fire, theft, hail. (Be aware that coverage for flood damage requires specific underwriting.) Usually, a home owner's policy is the least expensive way to insure a dwelling.

When you buy home owner's insurance, you need to be aware of the difference between actual cash value insurance and guaranteed [true] replacement value. Actual cash value refers to the depreciated value of the items; guaranteed replacement means your contents and structure will be 100 percent replaced. Guaranteed replacement is usually worth its small additional cost.

Dwelling Insurance

Dwelling insurance, although not as comprehensive as home owner's insurance, may be just as expensive. Because of age, condition, or location, some dwellings are not insurable under home owner's policies.

Renter's Insurance

Renter's insurance covers the value of your furniture and other possessions for replacement. It also provides liability coverage if someone is hurt as a result of your negligence or the negligence of your children. An example of this is someone falling over a toy or slipping outside of the home.

Umbrella Liability Insurance

An *umbrella liability policy* gives you extra coverage not provided by your auto and home owner's policies.

People with a large net worth or an occupation with a lot of public exposure may be wise to have additional coverage in our sue-happy society. It is more likely to be needed as the result of a car accident than an incident in the home, but an umbrella policy covers liability for a broad range of risks.

Automobile Insurance

Most states require *liability insurance* on all cars. This type of insurance covers the damage a driver might cause to others in an accident.

Everyone should carry at least liability insurance whether the state requires it or not. Potential liability is great, and the cost of liability insurance is relatively small.

One "at fault" accident can put a family in debt for life. Remember, *"The prudent sees the evil and hides himself, but the naive go on, and are punished for it"* (Proverbs 22:3).

Full Coverage

Full coverage on a vehicle includes all basic coverages: bodily injury, liability, property damage, medical payments, uninsured motorists, collision, and comprehensive.

Full coverage is worth considering on a newer car; some lenders even require it. It is often offered as part of the loan package, but it's usually best to buy it directly from the insurance company or agent.

Bodily Injury Liability

This pays for injuries to other people or for their death as the result of an accident involving your car. It covers people in other vehicles, guests in your car, and pedestrians, regardless of who is driving your car.

Coverage under this type of policy uses terms like "100/300." The first number is the amount in thousands that the policy will pay for one person. The second number is the amount in thousands that it will pay for all persons involved in an accident.

Property Damage Liability

This portion of the insurance policy covers damage to property caused by your car. Covered property includes such things as houses, buildings, fences, livestock, and any other property belonging to someone else.

The terms of coverage are expressed as "50/100/25." Each number represents thousands and is the maximum the insurance company will pay. The first number is the amount paid for each person injured; the second number is for each accident; and the third number is for property damage.

Personal Injury Protection

This will pay benefits to injured persons for medical expenses, lost wages, substitute services (if someone is unable to take care of his or her household), and death, no matter whose fault the accident was.

The protection is in effect whether a person is riding in or on your vehicle, getting in or out of it, or is struck as a pedestrian.

Medical Payments Coverage

This covers medical expenses that result from accidental injury to anyone riding in your vehicle or to anyone struck as a pedestrian.

Collision Insurance

Collision insurance pays for damages to your vehicle if you are involved in a collision. It does not cover the vehicles of anyone else involved in the accident.

Usually, a deductible is written with this coverage. And the company will pay only the market value of your car if there's an accident.

For example, suppose you have a six-year-old compact car with a market value of $1,000. You're involved in an accident that causes $2,500 in damage to your car. Instead of receiving $2,500 to fix your car, you would receive only $1,000 minus your deductible. If you had a deductible of $500, you would get only $500 ($1,000-500) to take care of the $2,500 damage.

You can see why it often does not pay to keep collision coverage on a car more than three years old unless it is a very expensive car.

Depending on your financial situation, you may be able to "self-insure" an older model car. Just set aside the value of the car into an interest-bearing savings account—to be used in the event your car is damaged.

Comprehensive Physical Damage Insurance

This provides for the replacement of glass and losses that result from anything but collision, such as fire, theft, vandalism, and hail. It is relatively inexpensive.

The cost of this coverage doesn't vary much with the car's age. Make the decision based on your budget. If the cost is very high for your income, carry liability only.

Uninsured Motorists

This covers injuries to you and your family caused by a hit-and-run driver or one who doesn't have liability insurance.

Other Coverages

Death and dismemberment insurance covers you or your family if there's a death or loss of a limb in an automobile accident.

Towing insurance pays part or all of the towing charges if your car breaks down.

Rental car reimbursement provides you with a car while yours is being repaired.

No Automobile Insurance—Faith or Foolishness?

Proverbs 27:12 has the answer to this question. It says, *"A prudent man sees evil and hides himself, the naive proceed and pay the penalty."* If you don't look ahead to see the evil and protect yourself, you will end up paying a penalty.

In most states, driving without liability insurance is not just bad judgment; it's illegal. You can go to jail for it, and your house and car can be taken if you hit somebody and can't pay the damages.

If you choose to disobey the law, you are willfully disobeying both the law and God's Word. *"Every person is to be in subjection to the governing authorities. For there is no authority except from God, and those which exist are established by God"* (Romans 13:1).

Liability insurance protects those who might be injured as the result of an accident you caused. If your "living by faith" shifts the risk to others, you are not living by faith; instead, you're forcing them to accept risk for something that they shouldn't have responsibility. Make the choice to be a blessing to others, and God will bless your willingness to be kind and thoughtful in this way.

Automobile Insurance for Teens

Whether a teenager owns a car or not, the issue of insurance must be addressed. Almost every insurance company will raise parents' insurance rates as soon as their sons or daughters are 16 and become licensed.

Remember what Proverbs 29:17 says, *"Correct your son, and he will give you comfort; he will also delight your soul."*

Most parents use their teenagers to shuttle other children back and forth. If you do the same, you need to set some very fundamental rules for the use of the car, for buying the insurance, and for maintenance.

Don't wait until your children become teenagers to begin training them for this serious responsibility. By taking extra time with them and preparing early in their training process, you will have more peace of mind and more trust as they take on more responsibility.

HELP *How to Save on Automobile Insurance Costs*

We've already seen that the age of your car and your ability to "self-insure" can reduce insurance costs. But taking advantage of discounts will also reduce cost.

Discounts are offered for:

1. good students with a B average or above
2. successfully completing a driver's education course
3. taking advantage of a carpool

4. multi-car families
5. students away at college
6. air bags
7. antitheft devices
8. senior citizens
9. farmers
10. defensive drivers
11. nonsmokers or nondrinkers
12. females age 30 to 64 who are the sole drivers.

You should check with your insurance agent to see if you qualify for any of these discounts.

It's also much cheaper for you to add a teenager to your insurance policy than to buy a separate policy. Limiting teenagers to a small percentage of the total use of the family car can lower your rates.

Anyone will save money by avoiding traffic violations. Speeding or ignoring traffic signs puts points on your driving record and adds dollars to your premiums.

In addition, the type of automobile you drive affects your premiums. If you drive a sporty or fancy car, you can expect to pay higher premiums.

Be sure to let your agent know immediately when circumstances change within your family. Review your coverage annually.

Other Types of Insurance Coverage

Long-Term Care Insurance

The majority of older people live in retirement homes or in their own homes because they are able to take care of themselves. But for those who need nursing home care, the expense can be enormous.

The cost of *long-term care (LTC) insurance* must be weighed against your ability to pay the premiums and the probability that you'll need such insurance.

If an indigent person needs nursing home care, the state will care for him or her with our tax dollars. But the Lord says we are to honor our fathers and mothers.

The word "honor" implies financial help. The long-term solution for our society is for us to take care of our older family members (1 Timothy 5:8).

Remember, if you can't afford insurance, then you have to believe God will take care of your needs another way.

Since *LTC insurance* is a relatively new field, treat it with even more care than you would give to other kinds of insurance. Search the Internet using the words "long-term care insurance" for current information.

The Consumer Law Page (http://consumerlawpage.com) contains plentiful advice, concluding that "long-term care policies are only for people with significant assets. . . ."

They also warn that very high commissions for LTC insurance policies result in pressuring vulnerable seniors to buy policies they cannot afford to maintain, noting that "far too many policies are cancelled by policyholders on fixed incomes as they grow older and their premiums increase accordingly."

Perhaps most sobering are these lines: "If you cannot afford to hire a lawyer to interpret the contract you want to buy, you should ask yourself if you can afford to buy coverage and, once you are in poor health and look forward to receiving policy benefits, whether you then will be able to pay for a lawyer to enforce your rights under the contract if benefits are not forthcoming. . . . Despite the claims of sales personnel, most policies are so flawed that if agents were honest about the policies' limitations, many customers would probably not purchase them at all."

Funeral and Burial Insurance

The best plan in existence to reduce burial costs is called the Funeral Consumers Alliance. When a family member dies, the Alliance guarantees burial at a very low cost.

The plan offered is through a standard funeral home. For more information, visit their Web site at funerals.org.

A second way to reduce burial costs is to visit your local funeral home in advance of death and prepay the funeral expenses. If you have a burial plot and pay for it before death, the cost is much less.

A third way to reduce burial costs is to donate your body to a medical school. The medical school will use the corpse for experiments and will provide burial at no cost.

Section 2

HEALTH AND DISABILITY INSURANCE

Today, health insurance is a basic need. Few families can afford the cost of even one hospital stay. So, medical insurance represents good, logical planning for most of us. It also makes good health care possible for families that otherwise couldn't afford it.

Health insurance is too complex to be discussed thoroughly in this small book, and significant changes in the health insurance industry are possible in the near future. Consult a professional for advice if your family is not covered by a plan provided by your employer.

Managed Care Plans

In recent years we have seen a major movement to *managed-care-type plans*. The goal of these plans, which are offered by many insurance companies, is to cut costs by negotiating a reduced charge with physicians and hospitals. These plans are more commonly known as Health Maintenance Organizations (HMOs), Preferred Provider Organizations (PPOs), and Point of Service plans (POSs). As managed care continues to evolve, we will see many variations of these managed care plans.

Health Maintenance Organizations (HMOs)—HMOs negotiate with major employers to take care of all their health care needs—from surgery to minor care. But the employers must use the HMO's doctors, hospitals, and clinics.

Preferred Provider Organizations (PPOs)—PPOs are similar to HMOs from the standpoint of negotiated charges. The main difference is that you can choose the physician you want to see. There are member and nonmember physicians and hospitals. If you choose a member provider, then your out-of-pocket expenses will be less than if you choose a nonmember provider.

Point of Service Plans (POSs) —These plans allow an insured person to choose his or her primary physician. This physician will have agreed to discounted fees for services rendered. The insured then would have to see this physician for all ailments first in order to receive the highest discount. If the insured decides to see a specialist on his or her own, the out-of-pocket expenses will be greater.

Medicaid

Medicaid pays medical bills for low-income people who can't afford the costs of medical care. It is a government-sponsored program with strict guidelines for eligibility. To find out if you qualify, contact your local public health or welfare office.

Medicare

Medicare is a government sponsored health insurance program for people who are 65 or older. Some disabled people also qualify.

It is a two-part program. Part A provides hospital benefits for short-term illness. It also provides some benefits for care in a skilled nursing facility or at home.

Individuals 65 or older who don't qualify for Medicare can still receive it by paying a monthly premium, which is adjusted each year.

Part B of Medicare is optional medical insurance, which is available for a small fee each month. You may have the premium automatically deducted from your Social Security benefit check, if you receive one. Part B pays most of your medical and surgical fees. It is an excellent value because it is so inexpensive.

Is Medicare Supplemental Insurance a Good Buy?

Medicare supplemental insurance is designed to take up where Medicare leaves off. It is relatively inexpensive for the amount of coverage it provides.

A good supplemental insurance policy should cover the whole range of health problems. Using a number of policies to cover specific illnesses is usually more expensive.

When buying health insurance, be sure your agent lists all preexisting conditions. This will help you avoid being disqualified if you file a claim.

Your supplemental policy should provide for long-term custodial care, such as nursing home care or care at home. In addition, it should give you the option of using facilities other than those approved by Medicare.

Also look for a shorter deductible period and a shorter waiting period for preexisting conditions. As always, compare policies and prices before you buy anything.

What If You Can't Afford Insurance?

This is a major concern when it comes to any type of insurance—but especially health insurance. Some people aren't covered by a group health plan, and they can't afford an individual plan or major medical plan. Their basic needs have to be met by God's people. This doesn't mean God can't provide, but He sometimes provides through His people.

If you don't have insurance at work and can't afford to buy it yourself, consider doing the following. Look for an inexpensive major medical plan with a high deductible that will pay for catastrophic illnesses. You may consider taking this plan to your Christian employer and asking if the company will pick up the cost.

If not, go to your church fellowship and present the plan as a legitimate need. If they don't respond, then you and your spouse should pray about it and decide if you are where God wants you to be.

Another option is to pay your own medical and dental bills. Many medical professionals will be happy to work something out with you. You may be able to clean their offices or find another way to work off what is owed. Do not avoid or run away from medical bills. God will help you find a way to handle them.

Summary

When planning your health insurance program, be sure the coverage fits your needs and your budget. Examine your policy carefully. Know which expenses are covered by your insurance and which are not.

Don't duplicate coverage. Some companies won't pay if you have another policy for the same coverage.

Look over your policy every year to be

sure it fits your family's current needs. Be sure you are covered against major expenses when funds are limited. Compare policies and costs. They vary greatly from one company to another.

Disability Insurance

Psalm 37:25 says, *"I have been young and now I am old, yet I have not seen the righteous forsaken or his descendants begging bread."*

Maintain a balance when buying insurance. Trying to insure yourself against every contingency can rob your family of needed funds and the blessing of God's provision. Still, the possibility of being disabled and unable to work is a situation you should address.

Depending on your level of disability, you may qualify for disability benefits from Social Security. Like other Social Security benefits, disability is based on the amount of Social Security taxes you've paid into the system.

Among all Social Security programs, disability is one of the most complicated. Therefore, it would be wise to become more familiar with the program by obtaining a free copy of the booklet, *Disability*, from your local Social Security office (SocialSecurity.gov).

Many employers provide a form of disability protection through a group plan. Find out if your employer offers this coverage.

In summary, pray about this decision and trust Him to show you the answer for your specific situation. He cares deeply for your well-being and wants the best for you and your family.

Section 3

LIFE INSURANCE

The purpose of *life insurance* is to continue providing for your dependents if you die. A reasonable calculation of their needs will reveal a target amount of insurance benefit that your policies should provide.

The Benefits of Owning Insurance

Most primary wage earners in a home need the greatest amount of life insurance when they're young—especially if they have a spouse and children at home who probably couldn't support themselves after the death of provider.

Insurance is used to produce the needed income; in that way it becomes a substitute for the breadwinner. To repeat Proverbs 27:12, *"A prudent man sees evil and hides himself, the naive proceed and pay the penalty."* The insured is looking ahead, seeing a potential problem and providing for it before it occurs.

Second, insurance frees surplus funds. Let's assume that the primary wage earner makes $35,000 a year. If this person dies, the family will need a $35,000 income. Let's further assume that Social Security will provide $15,000 a year for dependent care. The family is still $20,000 a year short. Where will the funds come from? It would take about $340,000 in assets, invested at 6 percent, to provide the $20,000 that the family still needs to survive.

These funds can be provided by saving $340,000, in which case insurance is not necessary, or by purchasing life insurance.

Even if a couple has $340,000, they may want to use the money to buy a home or for other purposes. If so, buying insurance would free the money for other use.

The Liabilities of Owning Insurance

One liability of insurance is that it costs money: You must reduce current spending to provide for the future.

Another liability of insurance is that it can divert your dependency from God. Solomon wrote, *"Trust in the Lord with all your heart and do not lean on your own understanding. In all your ways acknowledge Him, and He will make your paths straight"* (Proverbs 3:5-6).

This doesn't mean we must avoid insurance, but it does mean that God, not insurance, should be the object of our trust. Choose to trust God first as you make decisions about insurance, knowing that He will guide your decisions. Your salvation and relationship in Christ is your greatest insurance policy!

Term Life Insurance

Term insurance provides coverage for a specific period of years. This period of years is known as a "term," and when the term ends coverage must be renewed.

Most term policies do not build any cash reserves, but they provide the greatest amount of death protection for your dollar. Term insurance is strictly for protection. In order for it to pay benefits, the policy must be in effect when you die.

Term premiums are based on age, with the cost going up as you get older. If you're going to buy term insurance, remember these four things.

1. Buy only what you need.
2. Be sure the policy is renewable to at least age 90.
3. Be sure it won't be canceled due to your bad health.
4. Compare its cost for a 20-year period to other kinds of insurance, such as whole life.

If you find that term insurance is best for your needs, seek counsel about the various policies before buying one from a professional Christian insurance agent.

Cash Value Insurance

Cash value insurance is known by a variety of names, including whole life, universal life, variable life, single premium life, and variable adjustable life. It is usually purchased for an individual's lifetime and, as more and more premiums are paid, the policy builds cash value.

Interest is earned on the cash value, just like money invested in a bank. Many times the policy also will pay dividends (cash returns), which can be used to offset the cost of insurance.

The most basic type of cash value insurance is **whole life**. A young person buying whole life, or some other type of cash value insurance, would pay higher premiums than for term insurance. However, one benefit of some cash value policies is that the premium never changes.

For young families on a tight budget, cash value insurance can be a major expense. At worst, it can be so costly that these families don't buy enough coverage at a time when their need is greatest.

Universal Life

Universal life is sometimes called "complete" and "total" life insurance. It is known by various names, including adjustable life and flex life. Universal life is a combination of term insurance and a tax-deferred savings account that pays a flexible interest rate.

That interest rate usually reflects current market rates. Therefore, it will be much higher than the savings rate of traditional insurance policies.

Universal life is broken down into three parts:

1. the death benefit,
2. administrative costs, and
3. the savings portion of the policy.

Some agents emphasize the savings you will accumulate by age 65. These agents are promoting the investment side of the plan. But, be sure the policy meets your primary goal, which may be maximum death benefit rather than accumulation.

Stated returns on your universal life policy will not begin to show until you have been paying premiums for 15 to 20 years. If you cancel the policy before this time, it will cost you dearly, compared to buying term insurance and investing the difference in a tax-deferred vehicle.

Variable Life Insurance

Several types of insurance, including universal life, whole life, and adjustable life, may also take the form of a *variable life insurance* policy.

A variable life policy is considered a security and is sold by prospectus. The death benefit and cash value go up or down depending on the investment vehicles chosen inside the policy. A variable life policy offers loan privileges, optional riders, and surrender and exchange rights, just as any other cash value policy does.

These new policies offer higher returns, but they also mean greater risk for policyholders. Returns can change drastically from year to year.

Sometimes the product that suits your needs best is actually a combination of things. That's what you get with variable life. It combines traditional insurance provisions with flexible administrative procedures. It also has investment features that compare with other market investments.

The Concept of Survivorship Life Insurance or Second-to-Die Life Insurance

Thanks to the Economic Recovery Tax Act of 1981, a husband and wife can postpone estate taxes until after they both die. This is done through a provision known as the Unlimited Marital Deduction.

This provides couples with increased flexibility during their lifetime. But in many cases, it places a substantial tax burden on their estate and its beneficiaries.

Survivorship life insurance is designed to address this need. Unlike traditional life insurance, which covers the life of one person, survivorship life covers two lives, with proceeds payable at the second death.

Reducing your estate tax burden is not the only use for a survivorship life policy. Other uses include the following.

- Key person insurance. This would apply to cases in which an employer could self-insure or absorb the loss of one key individual but not two.
- Business buyout. One example of this is the purchase of a family business from aging parents. A child working in the business owns the policy on the parents.
- Charitable gift replacement. This provides heirs with replacement cash when assets are used to fund a Charitable Remainder Trust.

Is Insurance a Good Way to Save?

One argument for cash value policies is that they "force" you to save money. After all, you must pay your premiums to keep the policy going, and the more you pay the more you save.

As a short-term investment, the savings in most insurance policies draw less than half the interest that can be earned elsewhere. It is a high price to pay for a lack of discipline.

Proverbs 19:20-21 tells us, *"Listen to counsel and accept discipline, that you may be wise the rest of your days. Many are the plans in a man's heart, but the counsel of the Lord, it will stand."*

Conclusions

A good way to determine the type of insurance you need is to consider two things:

1. the amount of insurance you need, and
2. the amount you can afford to pay.

Obviously, you need to consider the current annual cost of a policy. But you also need to consider the cost of that policy during the next 20 years.

Shop for the best policy that fits your individual needs at the lowest cost. The best value usually comes from buying term insurance and saving the difference in a deferred or tax-free investment.

Unfortunately, most people don't save the difference; they spend it. At the same time, their term insurance premiums increase as they grow older. Eventually, these premiums may become too expensive for them to afford.

In conclusion, term insurance plus savings provides the best value. However, if you haven't been disciplined enough to save the difference by age 35, convert to a whole life plan.

How Much Insurance Is Enough?

"There is a grievous evil which I have seen under the sun: riches being hoarded by their owner to his hurt" (Ecclesiastes 5:13). It's very important, especially for young families with children, to determine the proper amount of insurance for their needs. Among the considerations:

- The ages of your children. The younger they are, the longer they'll need to be supported if you die.
- The income capability of the surviving spouse. This is a major factor, particularly if that spouse is not working.

- Existing debts, current lifestyle, and any other sources of after-death income.

One person may want to supply enough insurance so that his or her family can live on the interest income. Another may wish to provide enough for a specific number of years. These decisions are important and should be made together by husband and wife.

A typical family's insurance needs begin when the first child is conceived. Those needs reach a maximum amount when the last child is conceived.

Another period when there's a greater need for insurance is when the children are grown and out of the home but the surviving spouse has not reached 62 years of age.

Unless he or she is disabled, the spouse won't qualify for Social Security survivor's benefits until age 62. Even then, the benefits will be reduced, because full benefits aren't paid until at least age 65.

If the spouse qualifies as disabled (based on Social Security's definition of "disabled") he or she can receive survivor's benefits as early as age 50.

The Life Insurance Needs Worksheet at the end of this chapter will help you determine an appropriate amount of insurance for your family situation.

Budgeting for Insurance

Once you've decided how much insurance you need, you must decide how much you can afford. Insurance should take no more than 5 percent of your Net Spendable Income (NSI). Net Spendable Income is the amount you have left after you've paid your tithe and taxes.

The 5 percent figure above does not include house or automobile insurance. It does include life insurance, health insurance, and disability coverage. Still, a 5 percent allotment for all these insurance needs is not very much. But we're assuming that you have health insurance as part of a group plan. Many people receive group health coverage through their employers, who pay a portion of the premiums, thereby reducing the cost to the employees.

If you're not part of a group health insurance plan, this percentage of your budget will increase, and you'll have to be very "choosy" about your life and health insurance plans.

If you increase the insurance area of your spending plan from 5 to 10 percent, then there is no alternative but to decrease another area to keep the total of percentages at 100.

Should Both Spouses Have Life Insurance?

In many families, both husband and wife are equal or nearly equal wage earners. When a family depends on both salaries, both spouses probably need to be insured. If one died or became injured, the family would be in deep financial trouble, possibly losing their home, cars, and virtually everything else they own.

If funds are limited, efforts should first be made to insure the primary wage earner. However, if there is a sufficient amount of money, insuring both husband and wife should be considered.

Should Children Have Life Insurance?

There are two logical reasons to have insurance on your children:

1. for burial expenses, and
2. to guarantee that they will be insurable in later years.

However, the only necessary reason is burial expenses. Making your children insurable is not usually necessary, since only a small fraction of people are uninsurable at the time they marry.

Things to Avoid When Buying Life Insurance

There can be a big difference between buying what you need and buying what an agent wants to sell you. So, if you're in the process of buying life insurance, consider the following advice.

1. Avoid the double indemnity clause, which pays double if you die in an accident. This is an extra expense for something you probably won't need. Most people die from causes other than accidents. If you're counting on double indemnity to provide enough insurance, you're gambling with your family's future. You should be sure you have enough insurance, regardless of how you die.
2. Forget premium waivers that pay your premiums for you if you become permanently disabled. They represent a large expense for a very small benefit.
3. Don't be pressured into buying insurance. Don't put it off unnecessarily, but take the time to learn what you need and what will provide the best value.

Pointers for Policyholders

1. Keep your company informed of your address. Each year a number of policyholders move without notifying their insurance companies. When you do this, you're taking a chance on having your policy lapse.
2. Read your life insurance policy. Your agent should be willing to help you. Be sure you understand the basic provisions and benefits.
3. Keep your policy in a safe place. You can get a duplicate policy if yours is lost or destroyed by fire but not without some inconvenience and delay.

   As an additional safeguard, keep a separate record of your policies. Be sure that your beneficiary knows where a copy of your policy is kept. Generally, policies must be sent to the company when you file for benefits.
4. Discuss your insurance program with your family or other beneficiaries.
5. Review your life insurance program with your agent once a year or when a major event occurs (birth, death, marriage, divorce).

No Insurance

God may direct some people not to have life insurance or any other after-death provision. However if you're married, both the husband and wife should agree on this decision—after they've prayed together and sought God's peace. If you have any doubts, go ahead and buy the insurance. You can always cancel it later.

Credit or Mortgage Life Insurance

Credit or mortgage life insurance is sold in connection with home, auto, or other credit extensions. It is the same as decreasing term insurance, which offers a steady premium but declining benefits.

This type of policy is designed to relieve survivors of economic strain by paying off the outstanding loan balance of the deceased. Credit disability insurance also covers monthly payments if you are disabled.

This is a relatively expensive form of insurance. Unless you are in a high-risk, hard-to-insure category, you're better off to increase your regular insurance to cover any mortgages or loans you have.

Final Note

This information is designed to cover basic biblical principles that apply to insurance. For more specific information, contact a Christian insurance agent in your community. In the event of any disputes or irregularities, you may contact your state insurance commissioner's office for assistance. And don't hesitate to contact Crown, particularly if you have questions that go beyond product and technical issues that are best answered by your agent or broker; and, we will refer you to someone who can answer your questions and concerns.

Just-in-time Insurance Avoids Double Loss

Grant and Lori Hudson

Grant and Lori Hudson lived in Air Force base housing (no rent or utility costs) on an officer's salary. Assured of a stable income, they spent freely. Ten years later they owned a house but had also spent their way to a $17,000 credit card balance.

Unfortunately, this was not their only problem. While Grant was away on a long deployment, Lori's need for emergency kidney surgery and a legal issue regarding the sale of their house left them with an empty savings account, $62,000 in debt, and no house.

When Grant returned home from his deployment, he went to a financial counselor, who advised him to file for bankruptcy. But a friend introduced the couple to Crown Financial Ministries. They called for help and applied many of the biblical principles from the materials they purchased.

Lori and Grant worked out a repayment plan with their creditors and avoided bankruptcy, relieving some of their stress. This was a blessing, because Grant began to have problems with his job. He was passed over for a promotion to the rank of major on two occasions and finally accepted a contract with the Air Force that allowed him to continue as a captain with a severe salary cut. Still, with God's help, he and Lori continued to repay debt, build a savings account, and build a college account for their children.

Five years later, Grant's aunt passed away and left part of her estate to him.

As a result, the couple received an unexpected check in the mail that covered the entire balance of their debt.

Things had definitely improved, but Lori was concerned about their insurance. "My husband had not been a believer in insurance," she says, noting that he only had a $50,000 life insurance policy through the Air Force. "He would get testy if I tried to discuss it with him."

But one day, while driving down the road, Lori and Grant tuned in to the Crown's radio broadcast and heard them talking about insurance. "I can remember sitting in that passenger seat and saying, 'Lord, please let him hear this!'" Lori says. "I had prayed so hard about it." Grant, however, seemed to pay no attention to the message and said nothing about it to Lori.

Within less than a month, Grant suffered a fatal aneurysm in the parking lot at the base after a late-night flying mission.

When representatives from the base arrived at Lori and Grant's house the following morning, one of their first questions was, "Did he have insurance?"

Lori didn't know, but Grant's commander was certain that Grant had provided for his family. "That man told me a month ago that he'd heard a radio broadcast about insurance and financial planning," the commander told Lori. "I know that man took care of you."

The commander ordered two men to conduct a search, and they found that only 17 days before his death, Grant had increased his insurance from $50,000 to $200,000.

"Crown taught my husband how to love his family in life," Lori says, "and how to love us at death."

Today, one passage of Scripture that is very precious to Lori is Psalm 27:13-14. It illustrates how God has worked in her life and met her needs. *"I am still confident of this: I will see the goodness of the LORD in the land of the living. Wait for the LORD; be strong and take heart and wait for the LORD"* (NIV). ■

You don't have to know it all!

This volume of information may seem overwhelming—more than you ever wanted to know. Don't worry: You don't need to grasp it all immediately, and you never have to become an expert unless it's your occupation.

The combination of this basic insurance information and the biblical principles that apply to it will enable you to make wise decisions for the welfare of your family. Make prayer the centerpiece of your decision-making process. *"Be anxious for nothing, but in everything by prayer and supplication with thanksgiving let your requests be made known to God. And the peace of God, which surpasses all comprehension, will guard your hearts and your minds in Christ Jesus"* (Philippians 4:6-7). God's peace is more valuable than anything we could ever buy.

Listen to Crown's *MoneyLife*™ radio program for daily wisdom on the topics of insurance, investing, and a host of other practical concerns. We're all in this together!

HOPE Your Response

So what do I do now?

On the next page, we encourage you to write at least one Action Step in response to the chapter you have just read. If you write more than one, prioritize them in a logical order so you have a clear first step that you can begin immediately.

Action Steps

We also encourage you to reward yourself for every Action Step completed. Since the enemy ("the accuser") will discourage you by making the journey seem impossibly long, you need to see each step as its own victory. Your progress will be faster and more enjoyable if you take a little time to celebrate it.

Your celebration doesn't have to take a lot of time or money to be meaningful. Just make it something you enjoy, and tie it to the Action Step you have completed.

Celebration Plan

Life Insurance Worksheet

Date ______________________________

Sample

GROSS MONTHLY INCOME			
Present annual income needs:	$ 53,280		
Subtract deceased person's needs:	$ 9,000		
Subtract other income available: (Social Security, investments, retirement)	$ 10,000		
= Net annual income needed:	$ 34,280		
Net annual income needed, multiplied by 12.5 (assumes an 8% after-tax investment return on insurance proceeds):		$ 428,500	
LUMP SUM NEEDS			
Debts:	$ 8,000		
Education:	$ 20,000		
Other:	$ 0		
Total lump sum needs:		$ 28,000	
TOTAL LIFE INSURANCE NEEDS:			$ 456,500

GROSS MONTHLY INCOME			
Present annual income needs:	$ ________		
Subtract deceased person's needs:	$ ________		
Subtract other income available: (Social Security, investments, retirement)	$ ________		
= Net annual income needed:	$ ________		
Net annual income needed, multiplied by 12.5 (assumes an 8% after-tax investment return on insurance proceeds):		$ ________	
LUMP SUM NEEDS			
Debts:	$ ________		
Education:	$ ________		
Other:	$ ________		
Total lump sum needs:		$ ________	
TOTAL LIFE INSURANCE NEEDS:			$ ________

Once you have quantified your approximate life insurance needs, deduct the amount of your present life insurance coverage to determine whether you need additional life insurance. Then analyze your spending plan to determine how much new insurance you can afford. Seek counsel to decide the precise amount and type of insurance that would meet your needs and spending plan.

CHAPTER 2 INVESTING

Section 1

TEN KEYS TO SUCCESSFUL INVESTING

Tom Hunter was a well-known Christian leader who believed God had given him a revelation about how to solve America's oil problems. It was 1980, at the height of the Arab oil embargo, and commuters throughout the nation were feeling the pinch of skyrocketing prices at the gasoline pump.

Tom claimed that he had been approached by an angel who revealed the location of hidden American oil deposits. These deposits, in an area where no oil had ever been discovered, defied all geological patterns established by the petroleum industry.

Despite the evidence contradicting his claim, Tom remained convinced that his revelation was true. He set out to raise the $3 million needed to drill in this spot, beginning with $50,000 from people in his church to do a prospectus and brochures.

He wanted to offer stock in the venture but was unable to obtain the necessary registrations. In Tom's opinion, satanic forces within several state governments had blocked the registrations. So, he offered stock anyway. With the help of two associates, Tom was able to raise nearly $600,000 from Christians who heard about the oil-drilling venture. Several families borrowed against their homes, and one 80-year-old couple risked their entire savings in the project.

The hole was dry and all the funds were lost. Lawsuits flew like snowflakes as disgruntled Christians sued one another, in violation of Paul's teachings in 1 Corinthians 6. The media picked up on the lawsuits because many elderly people had been duped into investing. As a result, the cause of Christ suffered disgrace in many communities as the venture's promoters were prosecuted, convicted, and given prison sentences.

These weren't stupid people—neither the promoters nor the investors. And they were probably no greedier than average; the promise of unusually high returns influences many to throw money at speculative ideas without careful research. Most of them—particularly the older investors—hoped for enough gain to achieve peace. That was their first mistake.

More money is not a bad thing, but it is not the source of peace. True peace comes only from God. *"Peace I leave with you; My peace I give to you; not as the world gives do I give to you. Do not let your heart be troubled, nor let it be fearful"* (John 14:27).

Find the Right Balance

Investing is not unscriptural. In fact, in the Parable of the Talents (Matthew 25:14-30), God gave to the stewards according to their abilities and directed them to manage their portions well. Each was rewarded or punished according to his stewardship.

We should distinguish between investment performance and investment purpose. Performance will vary based on our response to constantly changing factors beyond our control. Increased knowledge and discipline should lead to increased skill and better performance.

Investment purpose, however, is not a matter of skill; it is a matter of intent. This is the foundation for the spiritual and moral side of the equation. As you learn to invest money according to God's principles, you'll find that God will increase your opportunity to help other people. That, in reality, is the true purpose of godly investing: to increase your assets so that you can serve God more fully.

Allowing material assets to erode through bad management is not good stewardship. It's a sign of laziness and poor stewardship. But if you simply multiply and store assets without purpose, you'll be guilty of hoarding—like the rich fool in Luke 12:16-21.

The 10 keys to successful investing are common principles that provide a solid foundation for any investor regardless of differing needs.

Key 1: Formulate Clear Investment Goals

No one should invest without having an ultimate purpose for the money. Whether it is for education, starting a business, retirement, etc., you should have a clear financial goal. Let's look at some common goals.

Retirement Goal

Even if you plan to continue working past 65, you may not be able to be as productive at that age. If you have to take a job that pays less than you need to live on, you'll need retirement savings to supplement your income. If you have enough in your retirement account to provide all the income you need, your work choices do not have to be dictated by financial necessity. Instead, they can reflect your heart and passion.

If your retirement goal is to someday sit down, kick up your heels, and do nothing, we would recommend a better goal. We believe it is beneficial to remain active after 65, especially when you have the freedom to work as a volunteer for a non-profit or Christian organization. Our Christian service doesn't end at 65. In fact, retirement years provide outstanding opportunities to advance God's work.

We recommend becoming debt-free, including your home mortgage, as your first investment goal in preparing for retirement. Once you've achieved that goal, you will be in a stable position to accelerate other investment vehicles.

The exception to this would be a company retirement account that matches your contributions. This benefit is too good to pass up if you can possibly afford it. Contribute up to the maximum amount your company will match, and allow any additional surplus in your spending plan to go toward mortgage reduction.

With your home paid off, you can start preparing for retirement and/or your children's college education with the money you were paying each month on your mortgage.

It takes discipline to invest this money, but it makes sense. You can't depend on Social Security to be your sole retirement plan; it was never intended to be anything more than a supplement to your retirement income.

Proverbs 6:6-8 says, *"Go to the ant, O sluggard, observe her ways and be wise, which, having no chief, officer or ruler, prepares her food in the summer and gathers her provision in the harvest."* It may seem that the "harvest" years of your life will stretch on forever, but remember that the winter years are coming. God will provide the means to save for the future as you trust Him.

Education Goal

Unlike those who are trying to preserve a windfall, a couple planning for their children's education may have to think more in terms of growth. This depends on the amount available to invest and the time in which it can be invested.

Let's assume, for instance, that a couple can put aside $1,000 a year for the education of their children, who will reach college age in about 10 years. With an interest rate of 5 percent and an inflation rate of 3 percent, at the end of 10 years they will have a little over $12,000. This will not be enough to educate one child, much less two or three. They will need to take some additional risks to achieve the growth they require.

This is the principle of "risk versus return," and we'll be dealing with it again and again. The higher the rate of return you need, the greater the degree of risk you'll have to assume.

Growth Goal

Some people need more growth potential in their investments. But there are others who seek a lot of growth potential because they're hoping to get rich quick. These people are willing to take big risks in an effort to become rich overnight. But Proverbs 28:22 says, *"A man with an evil eye hastens after wealth and does not know that want will come upon him."*

Tax Shelter Goal

This goal is very complex. Tax laws constantly change, and the average investor has few shelters left beyond depreciation and interest.

Beware of the common perception that paying interest is a good tax shelter. When you pay interest to save income tax, you lose and the lender gains.

On the other hand, depreciation and investment tax credits can be legitimate tax shelters. But an important principle to remember is that when you "defer" income tax through depreciation, you eventually must recapture it. Most tax shelters don't really eliminate income tax; they only defer it to a later time.

Key 2: Avoid Personal Liability

Many get-rich-quick schemes, as well as many tax shelters, are available only if you accept personal liability for a large debt. God's Word warns against "surety," which means making yourself personally liable for indebtedness without a sure way to repay.

For example, suppose you wanted to

buy a piece of property for $10,000 but had only $2,000 as a down payment. You put your $2,000 down on the property and then sign a note for $8,000 that says, "If I can't pay the note, the lender has the right to recover the property and sue me for any deficiency." Although the note is not likely to use these exact words, the fine print generally contains the described provision. This is surety.

On the other hand, let's assume you buy the same $10,000 piece of property with the same $2,000 down payment, and sign a different note for $8,000. This one reads, "If I can't pay the note, the lender has the right to recover the property and keep what I've already paid, but I owe nothing additional."

The second note involves no personal liability for any deficiency. The legal term is *non-recourse* or *exculpatory* debt, meaning you have limited your liability to the collateral at risk. This avoids surety because you always have a sure way to pay: surrendering the property.

Avoid personal liability. Then, if you buy equipment, property, or investments, the most you can lose is the money you have "at risk," not future earnings. Failure to do this can result in the total loss of all your family's assets. Investments that go bad often do so during the worst times in the economy, the very times when you are least capable of carrying the loss.

Illustration. *Ron and Stan were doctors who invested together in numerous real estate ventures. One of these investments was an apartment complex, which had been offered for about half of its appraised value. The deal had required* *a $1 million mortgage with a minimal down payment of only $50,000.*

Both men were assured that there was no way the investment could go bad. After all, they could make money with the complex only 50 percent occupied, and it had never been less than 80 percent occupied. The only hitch was that they had to personally endorse the note. In other words, they personally guaranteed the lender against any losses.

About two years later it was discovered that the complex had urea formaldehyde insulation in the ceiling and walls. It was condemned, and health officials required that the entire structure be torn down.

The insurance paid for a portion of the loss, and Ron and Stan were able to sell the land for another portion. But they were still personally liable for nearly half a million dollars. Ron went bankrupt. Stan, who was a Christian, felt it would not be right to go bankrupt and committed to repay the loan. ■

The investment itself was good—barring the unknown health hazard—and the deal was excellent. The problem was that Ron and Stan entered into surety by signing for personal liability. Remember the wisdom of Proverbs 22:26, which says, *"Do not be among those who give pledges, among those who become guarantors for debts."* Don't enter into surety, no matter how good the deal sounds.

Key 3: Evaluate Risk and Return

An important factor in investing is called the "risk versus return" ratio. The higher the rate of return, the higher the degree of risk. You can lower the risk by education and careful analysis, but you cannot eliminate it.

The reason an investment pays a higher rate of return is because it must do so to attract the needed capital. For example, an insured CD or a government note may pay 3.5 percent, but a corporate bond may pay 5.5 percent to 10.5 percent.

Why does a corporate bond pay a higher interest rate than a government note? Because the risk in corporate bonds is higher than in government notes. Before investing in anything riskier than an insured savings account, you need to ask yourself this fundamental question: "Can I really afford to take this risk?"

The answer to that question normally depends on two factors: age and purpose. The older you are, the less risk you can afford to take because it's more difficult to replace the money.

If the purpose of the money is for retirement or education and both are still years away, you can probably afford to take a higher risk.

However, if you need the investment funds to live on right now, then you need the lower risk, regardless of age. If you find an investment that promises a high rate of return with a low degree of risk, watch out; there's no free lunch.

As Proverbs 14:18 says, *"The naive inherit foolishness but the sensible are crowned with knowledge."*

Key 4: Keep Some Assets Debt Free

If you're using leverage (borrowed money) to fund some of your investments, keep at least 50 percent debt free. This also assumes you are following the guidelines of Key #2 and are not accepting surety. In other words, the money you have at risk in the investments is all you can lose. You have no contingent liability.

The basic idea behind this strategy is to leverage about half of your investments, expecting that the investment earnings on the money you borrow will be greater than the interest rate you pay to borrow it.

If you leverage no more than half of your investments and you lose them due to an economic downturn, the other half remain sound—provided you haven't entered into surety with the leveraged ones. Leveraging is better suited for experienced investors who know what they're doing. Even then, the risk can be high. It's not a good idea for the average investor, who doesn't have a large surplus.

Illustration. *Joe was a real estate developer whose business had suffered a large slump due to the economy in his area. He had no surety and had kept at least half of his assets debt free. This would enable him to sell his leveraged investments without losing everything.*

Joe's friends encouraged him to take their approach and sell some of his debt-free investments to help carry some others. He had tens of thousands of dollars in the other investments and didn't want to lose them.

His friends were risking good assets to feed their debts. They had very little choice, since they had personally endorsed every loan and everything was at risk. But Joe had a choice.

He was about to gamble that the economy in his area would turn around before his assets were exhausted. A wise counselor advised against risking good assets to feed loans. "If they can't pay their way or be sold, let them go," he said.

Joe followed this advice and is still in business, but most of his associates have failed. In fact, he was able to develop a new business: managing properties for insurance companies and banks that have foreclosed on heavily indebted real estate. ■

Key 5: Be Patient

How many investments have you seen advertised as really bad deals? Although bad ones abound, they all look good initially. And since most salespeople sincerely believe in their products, it's up to you to sort out the good from the bad. In your eagerness to get your money working for you, remember that patience will help you avoid many errors.

You must know what your goals and objectives are and only select the investments that help you meet them. Remember that greed and speed usually work together, which is why most get-rich-quick schemes require quick decisions. Let patience be your strong ally in defeating greed's bad choices.

It helps to recognize the strategies employed by get-rich-quick schemes. They all:

1. Attract people who don't know what they're doing. When you invest in areas that you know little about, it's difficult to evaluate a good or bad investment. Christians are often very gullible and prone to follow the recommendations of other Christians who don't know what they're doing either.

2. Encourage people to risk money they cannot afford to lose. Most people are more cautious with money they've earned than with money they've borrowed. Borrowed money comes so easily that it's easy to risk.

3. Pressure people to make investment decisions on the spot. Many get-rich-quick plans rely on group meetings and a lot of emotional hype. But if you hear of a deal that sounds so good that you don't want to wait and pray about it, pass it up. Good investments are rare and seldom flashy.

Illustration. Chad was a young computer salesman who reluctantly called Larry Burkett for counsel after his wife, Chris, pressured him into it. Here is Larry's account of the story.

"We have to see you right away," he said. "I've got a deal that's too good to pass up and I've got to move quickly." We scheduled a time for the following day.

When they arrived, Chad talked about a computer hotshot in Colorado who had developed a program to do stock market trades between the U.S. and European stock exchanges. Profits would be made on the differences between the two markets.

This "specialist" was taking investors and making over 10 percent per month for them. Chad had already cashed in his retirement plan and was about to borrow against the equity in their home. He calculated that he could make enough to start his own business in just two years.

Chris was panic-stricken at the thought of Chad risking $25,000 with someone he didn't even know. But Chad said he had talked with several other investors who were making lots of money. He said the software developer had paid exactly what he promised every month.

We asked, "Why does he need your money if he's able to make over 100 percent per year? Why doesn't he just borrow the money at 10 percent per year instead of paying out 10 percent per month?"

Chad answered, "He wants Christian investors so he can get into other ventures in the future."

Since any investment targeted primarily at Christians is worthy of some suspicion, we asked Chad if he would mind us checking out this person.

"No," he said, "but how long will it take? I've got to make a decision quickly or the opportunity will close."

Our counsel regarding biblical principles and get-rich-quick schemes fell on deaf ears. Chad had already made his decision. This appointment was just a necessary step to pacify his wife.

Our investigation found nothing on this computer trading genius. If he had learned his trade by handling stocks and bonds, nobody knew about it. We called to get a financial statement and were repeatedly assured that one was "on the way." But we could never get even the slightest documentation on what he was doing.

In the meantime, Chad invested $25,000 in this venture and received a $3,000 check for the first month's profits. The next month he was offered the option of reinvesting the profits, which he did over our objections. But when the third month rolled around, Chad's distribution never came.

The state securities commissioner impounded all the assets of the "trader," pending an investigation for securities fraud. He had not been trading stocks at all. He'd simply been raising money from gullible people—a lot of them.

The system was pretty simple—a classic Ponzi scheme. He paid dividends by raising more money each month. Once investors had received a month or so of distributions, they were "allowed" to reinvest their profits, which most did.

As long as the circle of investors kept expanding, the trader had no problems making the payments—and a huge profit. His only overhead was a computer to keep up with the payments.

The end came when an investor tried to talk his brother-in-law into investing. Fortunately, the brother-in-law was a security investigator who knew a scam when he saw one.

By the time this "stock trading" operation was shut down, it had raised more *than $20 million and had a list of clients that read like who's who in entertainment, sports, and business.* ■

As the Proverb says, *"A faithful man will abound with blessings, but he who makes haste to be rich will not go unpunished"* (Proverbs 28:20).

Get-rich-quick schemes always look great at the outset. If they didn't, no one would buy them. Be cautious and patient. *"Rest in the Lord and wait patiently for Him"* (Psalm 37:7). Before you do anything, talk about it, pray about it, investigate it, and give God time to answer.

Key 6: Diversify

The old adage that says, "Don't put all your eggs in one basket" certainly applies to your investment strategy.

Let's assume, for example, that you have $1,000 to invest and you want to buy some stock. If you put your $1,000 into one company's stock, then all of your money rests on how that one company's stock performs.

A good alternative is a mutual fund, where thousands of investors pool their money to buy stock in many different companies. This gives you immediate diversification.

You can achieve further diversification by splitting your investment into different areas of the economy. Real estate, gold and silver, stocks and bonds, CDs—all of these offer some advantages.

The probability is that when one of these areas is down, another will be up. So rather than having to sell the one that's down, you could sell one that's up.

Remember that Bernard Baruch said, "When everybody else is buying, it's time to sell." What you should strive to do is buck the trends, rather than be forced to go with them.

The current proliferation of mutual funds and exchange-traded funds (ETFs) enable you to diversify in ways that would have been impossible a few years ago. But don't make the mistake of thinking that owning shares of several mutual funds automatically means broad diversification. If the funds don't differ significantly in their investment strategy—the kinds of stock they hold—you could end up with several copies of the same thing. We'll talk more about mutual fund diversification later.

It is important to remember that the principle of diversification is not a one-time decision. In other words, we don't diversify and then forget it. Managing God's assets is a lifelong privilege and responsibility. If we lack knowledge, we should try to gain it. Spending an hour a day for six months studying any area of investing will teach us more than many investment salespeople know.

Key 7: Consider Long-range Bonds

Your investment program should take into account long-range economic trends, especially inflation. People who follow only short-range trends often get trapped.

When the economy is doing well and inflation and interest rates are down, people want to jump into the stock market and "make a lot of money." Some of them will make a lot but then panic during a short-term downturn and lose most or all of it.

People who speculate may wind up losing more than they made, especially if they borrow to invest. When the market drops, they can't afford to ride it out, so they sell in a down market, guaranteeing losses.

It is always important to take the long-term approach; whatever is going on right now will eventually reverse. Long-term thinking does not mean that your investments remain stagnant, but it does mean that you resist panic. Bernard Baruch noted that "most people tend to panic when their assets decline in value, and they will sell simply because they have not taken a long-range view of things."

Inflation and the government's attempts to control it are the most significant economic trends that affect investments.

The most inflation-proof investments over several decades have been real assets: things that you can use and touch, such as land, metals, apartment buildings, or houses—and stocks or funds that focus on real assets.

During periods when inflation and interest rates are down, many of the paper investments like stocks and bonds do very well. During this time, people tend to forget about inflation.

That can be a costly mistake in a debt-run economy. When inflation turns around and interest rates increase to combat it, years of growth can be wiped out in a few months.

Key 8: Focus on What You Own

Many people with significant net worth have been wiped out during economic downturns. We've counseled many who had looked great on paper but had highly leveraged assets requiring regular payments. When interest rates rose and the economy tightened, they couldn't keep up with the payments, and they lost everything, including their homes.

Illustration. Here's another account from Larry Burkett. Even in today's economy, you'll see that the only things that really change in these classic stories are the names, dates, and figures. History has a way of repeating itself!

We met an oilman in the late 1970s. He was a committed believer and a member of the Christian Oilmen's Association. He had gotten into the oil business just before the oil embargo and had seen the price of oil go from about $6 a barrel to over $30.

It seemed that everything he touched turned to gold, and he was thoroughly hooked on the Christian "prosperity message." He literally believed that his giving guaranteed him immunity from economic problems.

He was worth millions through oil leases and several drilling operations, but everything was leveraged to the limit. He used every increase in oil prices to borrow more against his reserves so that he could expand further.

When we challenged him on the principle of surety, he became very defensive and ducked behind the normal Christian escape: "God told me to do it."

He said he prayed regularly about every decision. Furthermore, he believed every increase in his assets was evidence that God was confirming his actions.

To make matters worse, he had adopted a good-economy mentality, believing that the economy would continue to inflate indefinitely and carry oil prices with it. He failed to realize that much of the inflation was due to increasing oil prices, which couldn't rise indefinitely.

Everything changed in the early 1980s, when the oil cartel fell apart and oil prices dropped. Newly elected President Reagan used high interest rates to curtail the money supply and bring inflation under control.

At the same time, higher oil prices encouraged worldwide conservation efforts that began to reduce the demand for oil. This triple blow crippled the oil industry.

Established companies like Shell, Texaco, and Gulf did well with their pre-inflation oil leases. But most of the new ventures got wiped out, including this Christian oilman.

He could have cashed out in 1979 with perhaps $20 million; yet in 1986, he saw his home and furnishings auctioned off by the court. ■

When we say focus on what you own, we mean what you own that is liability free. Highly leveraged assets may produce stunning returns over short periods of time when conditions are perfect, but they become time bombs when conditions change. Make it your goal to have at least half of your assets free of any debt. If you can't do that right now, make it your number-one long-range goal.

How can you do it? By saying, "The next time I sell an investment, I'll use the proceeds to pay off another investment." As the Lord said, *"For which one of you, when he wants to build a tower, does not first sit down and calculate the cost, to see if he has enough to complete it?"* (Luke 14:28).

Key 9: Know Where to Sell

Before you buy, always know where you can sell the investment. This key is very important when you're dealing with "exotic investments," such as gemstones, silver, gold, or collectibles.

You can do very well buying these items if you know what you're doing. But most people who buy collectibles have no idea of where or how to sell them.

For example, suppose that the precious metals market is doing very well and you want to sell an antique silver plate. Let's arbitrarily assume that silver is being quoted at $16 an ounce.

The first thing you discover is that your plate is probably worth a lot more than its silver content, based on what you paid for it as an antique. So the price quoted on silver has little meaning.

The market for your plate would be a collector and, normally, through an antique broker. Many novice collectors have discovered to their dismay that the price they paid for an object was retail—or more—and the price they're offered is wholesale—or less.

Let's assume that you bought gold in bullion form. Unless you have an agreement with the sales company that they will buy it back from you, you may have a difficult time finding a buyer.

If you decide to sell it, and gold is being quoted for $800 an ounce, you will discover that a broker won't give you $800 an ounce for it.

In fact, he may offer as little as $700 an ounce even though it's certified bullion. Why? Because he needs to make a commission on it too.

Other collectibles, such as figurines, paintings, stamps, and coins, are very difficult for a nonprofessional to sell profitably.

When you invest in these you need to have a clear understanding of how and where you can resell them. We've counseled many people who said, "Well, the salesperson told me that if I ever wanted to resell, he would buy it back."

But later they found that their salesperson was no longer around. Even businesses that have survived for 50 years can still fold, especially in a bad economy. It is vital to know you have a ready market without unacceptable transaction costs.

Usually investors are better off staying with less exotic investments that have multiple markets available.

Key 10: Train Family Members

Every family member should be trained in the principles of sound investing. This is critical for children because they'll eventually move away and be responsible for managing their own family's finances.

It's critical for wives because 85 percent of them will outlive their husbands. That's an important statistic to remember when developing an investment portfolio. People who don't understand investments often sell at the wrong time and suffer significant losses. Also, since it is not uncommon for a husband and wife to die together in an accident, the older children should be brought into decisions involving investments. At a minimum, leave instructions so they'll be able to manage your portfolio without having to dispose of it just to pay estate taxes after your death.

Section 2

DEVELOPING AN INVESTMENT STRATEGY

In order to gain a thorough understanding of the principles of investing, a few definitions are in order.

First, both income and growth may be included under the general term "return." In other words, you may have cash income from a certificate of deposit (CD), or you may have growth income from a rental house. Both are considered "return" on investment. The first is immediate and the second is long-term.

Income is the average current yearly yield. Growth refers to average yearly appreciation. So, if you get a 5 percent cash return from a rental house after all expenses are paid, and the house is also appreciating 5 percent per year, it has a 10 percent per year return on investment.

The term "risk" refers to potential loss. In other words, what is the probability that you will get your money back on an investment? Risks are numerous and vary with the type of investment. Let's use the relatively low-risk example of fixed-income securities. With this type of investment, the major sources of risk include the following.

1. **Interest rate risk.** Changes in interest rates can affect bond returns and bond prices.
2. **Purchasing power risk.** Over a period of time, inflation eats away at your purchasing power. The more severely inflation rises, the more severely your purchasing power is diminished.
3. **Market risk.** The market (in general) affects the price behavior of your securities.
4. **Marketability risk.** How easily can you sell a particular issue at or near prevailing market prices?
5. **Business risk.** If the issuer has large financial and operating risks, the risk of default is increased.
6. **Reinvestment risk.** This is your ability to reinvest your principal and/or coupon/ dividend receipts at a desirable rate.
7. **Call risk.** Your security may have a call feature that gives the issuer the right to prematurely retire the obligation. As a result, you may be forced to reinvest the funds in a lower-yielding investment.
8. **Price risk.** This particular risk is based on changes in interest rates. Depending on the maturity of your

obligation, price behavior may be affected to a lesser or greater extent. The longer it takes your obligation to mature, the more susceptible you are to this type of risk. Therefore, short-term obligations have less exposure to price risk when interest rates are rising.

In this section, we'll present some of the more common investments available and place them on a multi-tiered system. These investments are tiered according to *risk* and *return (income)*.

We have assigned a scale from 0 to 10 that can be applied to each type of investment. Zero represents the least risk or the least return, and 10 represents the highest risk or highest return.

Therefore, an investment with a return potential of 0 and a risk factor of 10 would represent the worst possible investment.

An investment with an income potential of 10 and a risk of 0 would be the best possible investment. (Unfortunately, they don't exist.)

We also have added a third factor: *growth*. Growth means the ability of an investment to appreciate (grow in value, such as common stocks).

Investments such as bonds have a potential growth factor also. If a bond pays a yield of 10 percent and interest rates drop to 8 percent, the bond value increases. If interest rates increase to 12 percent, the bond value decreases, resulting in negative growth or loss of capital.

We'll cover these five tiers:

1. Secure income investments
2. Long-term income investments
3. Growth investments
4. Speculative investments
5. High-risk investments

The ratings you'll see on the following investments represent an opinion, not an absolute fact. Times and economic conditions constantly change, and the degree of return or risk for most types of investments will fluctuate accordingly.

When interest rates and inflation are high, real property, residential housing, apartment complexes, or office buildings generally do well. But when interest rates and inflation are down, stocks and bonds generally do well.

Unfortunately, high and low are relative terms that are best gauged in the rear-view mirror—after it is too late to respond with certainty. And much of the time, interest and inflation are neither particularly high nor low; they are somewhere in the middle, trending in a direction. If you could guarantee even the direction in advance, the market would provide easy money, but market direction is never uniform or orderly. It is characterized by so many sudden changes that no daily chart is predictable. Line up 10 different experts and you'll get 20 plausible scenarios.

Tier 1: Secure Income Investments

Government Securities

(Income 5)(Growth 0)(Risk 1)

Treasury bills (T-bills), U.S. savings bonds, series E bonds, and Series I bonds all fall into this category. You can also buy shares of mutual funds that invest exclusively in T-bills or Ginnie Maes.

Bank Securities

(Income 5)(Growth 0)(Risk 3-4)

One advantage of bank investments like savings accounts, certificates of deposit (CDs), and insured money funds is that you can invest with smaller amounts of money; you can purchase a CD for as little as $500. The disadvantages are that they offer little or no growth because the payout is fixed and the income is taxable as it is earned.

Be certain that you invest with a bank or savings and loan protected by the FDIC or a credit union insured up to $100,000. In a worst-case scenario, the government will print the money to pay what it owes.

If you elect to tie up your money long-term and have a choice between a government security or bank note, the government security includes the safety of being a primary obligation of the government.

Money Funds

(Income 4-5)(Growth 0)(Risk 2-8)

Money funds are the pooled funds of many people. The funds are used to purchase short-term securities. These are not true savings accounts but are short-term mutual funds that pay interest.

Money funds are available through most brokerage firms, savings and loans, and banks; those offered by brokerage firms aren't federally insured against losses. Interest rates usually are adjusted monthly.

It's important to verify the rating of any money fund frequently. If the rating drops below "A," remove your money and select another fund.

Also, don't maintain more than $25,000 or 10 percent of your assets (whichever is lower) in any one money fund.

Tier 2: Long-Term Income Investments

Municipal Bonds

(Income 5)(Growth 0)(Risk 7-8)

These are bonds issued by a local municipality, usually a larger city like Houston or Hartford. The primary selling feature is that most or all of the income from municipal bonds is exempt from federal income tax (and state income tax in the state where they are issued).

The disadvantages of individual municipal bonds are: (1) they have low yields; (2) they normally require a large initial investment; and (3) there may not be a readily available resale market for them.

Mortgages

(Income 8)(Growth 0-5)(Risk 3-4)

A mortgage is a contract to lend someone money to buy a home or other real property. The lender (investor) holds the mortgage rights to the property until the loan is totally repaid.

One way to become a mortgage holder is to buy a mortgage through a mortgage repurchase agreement. These agreements are commonly offered by commercial lenders who want to resell loans they have made.

The seller normally discounts the mortgage to yield from 1 percent to 3 percent above the prevailing interest rates. So, if current interest rates on CDs are 7 percent, you can earn 8 percent to 10 percent through repurchased first mortgage loans.

The risk on this type of investment is relatively low because you have real property backing the loan. If a borrower fails to pay, you can foreclose on the property, but that requires a process beyond the interest and experience of average investors.

An important factor is the value of the property securing the mortgage. High-powered investment banks have lost billions through properties appraised at unrealistic prices and secured by high mortgages to unqualified buyers.

Corporate Bonds and Bond Funds

(Income 6-8)(Growth 0-3)(Risk 5-6)

A corporate bond is a note issued by a corporation to finance its operation. Quality bonds often yield 2 percent to 3 percent higher interest rates than an equivalent CD or T-bill.

The amount of return depends on the rating of the company issuing the bond. Bonds are rated from a low of C to a high of AAA. The higher the grade of the bond, the lower the rate of return, but the risk is lower as well.

Unfortunately, the rating of a company can change quickly. Most average investors would be better off using a bond mutual fund to achieve the long-term income they seek. The returns are slightly lower, but the risks are lessened through diversification in many companies' bonds.

Insurance Annuity

(Income 3-4)(Growth 0)(Risk 5-6)

This investment requires a prescribed amount of money to be paid into the annuity, and then the issuing insurance company promises a monthly income after retirement age.

The advantages of investing in annuities are as follows.

1. The earnings are allowed to accumulate, tax deferred, until you retire.
2. The investment is fairly liquid, so if you have to get your money out, you can, although there is often a penalty.
3. Compared to other tax-sheltered investments, the returns are good.

Be aware that the stated yield of an insurance annuity isn't necessarily what you will receive. Sometimes the percentage given is a gross figure from which sales and administrative costs are deducted.

It's best to ask for a net figure to do your comparisons. Get all quotes in writing from the agent offering the annuity.

Dividend-paying Stocks
(Income 4-5)(Growth 0-10)(Risk 6-7)

Common stocks usually pay dividends based on the earnings of the company. One advantage is that stocks can be purchased for relatively small amounts of money.

It's possible to invest in a stock paying a dividend of 7 percent to 8 percent and invest less than $100. This obviously appeals to the small investor. Since the dividend is totally related to the success of the issuing company, I would look for a company that has paid dividends for many years, particularly during economic hard times. Be aware, though, that just because a corporation has paid dividends for decades doesn't necessarily mean that it can continue to do so.

As stated previously, a good quality mutual fund can lessen the risk but achieve the same results. Professional management, together with broad diversification, provide a great advantage.

Tier 3: Growth Investments

This tier is in the middle and represents the crossover from conservative to speculative investments. During one cycle of the economy these investments may appear to be conservative, but then during the next cycle they could appear to be speculative.

Undeveloped Land

(Income 0-2)(Growth 6-7)(Risk 7-8)

During the highly inflationary '70s, farmland and other undeveloped properties were good investments. People speculated in land just as they did in income properties. This drove prices up and, unfortunately, tempted farmers to join the speculators.

The 1980s saw inflation subside and land prices level out. Consequently, raw land prices also fell. This scenario can and will change again as the economy changes in the future. Be sure that you find a trusted professional in this field to advise you.

Housing

(Income 5-7)(Growth 0-5)(Risk 3-4)

Housing costs are out of the price range of most average young couples, and since they have to live somewhere, most of them will rent, at least temporarily.

One advantage of investing in rental housing is that it can be done with a relatively small initial down payment. When investing in rental properties, the most important principle to remember is to assume no surety. If the house won't stand as collateral for its own mortgage, pass it by.

Rental housing not only generates income but also shelters much of that income through depreciation and interest deductions on taxes.

On the other hand, there are several negatives to consider before investing in rental housing.

1. If you don't want to be a landlord, don't buy rental housing.
2. If you have to pay someone to maintain and manage your properties, you give up a significant portion of the return.
3. It's not always easy to get your money out if you need it.

An alternative to investing in single-family rental housing is to invest in duplexes and triplexes. If you don't have the money to get into a duplex or triplex by yourself, there are two alternatives.

- You can invest in limited partnerships offered by individuals who purchase and manage duplexes and triplexes. Remember, however, that the managing partner has total control.
- You can invest with another person.

The advantage of owning a duplex or triplex is that your income isn't limited to one renter. With a single-family home, if your renter moves out, you have a 100 percent vacancy. But with a duplex you would still have 50 percent occupancy.

The liabilities with duplexes and triplexes are that they require a bigger investment and more maintenance, and you really do become a property manager.

Remember the three key factors about buying any rental property, whether it is a single-family house, duplex, or triplex: location, location, and location.

Mutual Funds

(Income 6-8)(Growth 4-5)(Risk 4-5)

A mutual fund is an investment pool for many small investors. A group of professional advisors invests for them, usually in the stock or bond markets.

There are specialized mutual funds that invest in precious metals, utility companies, government securities, and so forth. In fact, you can find a mutual fund for almost any area in which you want to invest.

Mutual funds are valuable for the small investor for several reasons.

1. You can invest with a relatively small amount of money (many mutual funds require as little as $500).
2. Your money is spread over dozens to hundreds of companies.
3. The return on the best mutual funds has averaged more than twice the prevailing interest rates for any 10-year period.

Potential investors in mutual funds should go to independent sources to check out the fund first. Since we are discussing growth mutual funds, it is important to verify the track record and projected earnings of any fund you might select. A prospectus from the mutual fund company will clearly define the "secure" or low-risk funds and the "growth" or speculative funds.

We prefer no-load (non-commission) funds because they don't subtract 5 percent or more from the initial investment.

If the performance of commission funds were substantially superior to no-load funds, the commission would be a non-issue. But the best no-load funds compare very well. Still, all funds have annual expenses that cut into the return. Make sure you evaluate these expenses (often 1 to 2 percent) as well as any penalties you will incur if you buy and sell shares too frequently.

Tier 4: Speculative Growth Investments

Common Stocks/Aggressive Growth Mutual Funds

(Income 2-8)(Growth 0-7)(Risk 7-8)

Again, the advantages of common stocks are that you can invest with a relatively small amount of money and the potential exists for sizable growth. The liabilities of common stocks are obvious.

First, you can suffer a loss as easily as you can make a profit. Second, stocks require some monitoring to maximize their potential. Buying and selling requires broker fees, although many discount brokers will execute computer trades for $7 to $15 per trade.

Discount brokers and computer trading have removed the liability of high commission costs and replaced it with a new liability: the lure of over-trading. When stock investing moves toward day trading, it becomes less investing and more gambling. Many people have lost large amounts of money through impatience and trying to score quickly.

Generally, it is more profitable and much less time consuming to use top-rated no-load mutual funds. If you want a fund that mirrors the Dow Jones Industrial Average or some other index, there are many such index funds from which to choose.

If you want one that will perform exactly opposite of the DJIA or some other index—rising when the index falls and vice versa—several are designed to do that. Just be aware that they will lose money most of the time because bull (favorable) markets generally last much longer than bear (unfavorable) markets.

Precious Metals

(Income 0)(Growth 0-8)(Risk 8-9)

As mentioned before, precious metals such as gold, silver, or platinum can be purchased either for long-term growth or pure speculation. For long-term growth, buy the metal, put it in a safety deposit box, and hope it appreciates over a period of time.

Most people do this primarily as a hedge against a potential calamity in the economy. A small percentage of your assets invested in precious metals can help to balance other assets more vulnerable to inflation.

Remember Bernard Baruch's advice, "When everybody else is buying, it's time to sell." Especially when it comes to precious metals.

Finally, keep a long-term mentality about precious metals—at least those you invest in as a hedge. And remember that gold and silver fluctuate with the economy. Gold usually cycles faster and further than silver, primarily because more people trade in it. In general, the cycles of gold run opposite the U.S. dollar; so, for clues to the price of gold, watch the dollar's trends.

Other speculative investments include limited partnerships, syndications, penny stocks, and collectibles. It is virtually impossible to assign a rating to these since they vary so greatly, depending on the investor's expertise. Suffice it to say that the risks are great and so are the potential returns.

The reason that many of these investments are shown in both the speculative and high-risk categories is because they fall into either, depending on what the economy is doing at the time.

Tier 5: High-Risk Investments

These investments should play only a relatively small part (5 percent to 10 percent at the most) in any investment plan. Their primary value is the potential appreciation; in other words, speculation. Most generate little or no income and are highly volatile.

Gold and Silver

(Income 0)(Growth 0-10)(Risk 9-10)

Not only can you invest in precious metals for long-term growth, but you can also invest in gold and silver for short-term speculation. This would be most beneficial in a highly volatile economy where major changes were occurring.

Obviously, such events are difficult to predict and are extremely risky. They are only for the investor with a strong heart and cash. Unless you are a professional investor, this probably is not an area in which you want to risk much money.

Oil and Gas

(Income 0-8)(Growth 0-10)(Risk 10+)

In the late 1970s and early 1980s, when crude oil prices cycled up, oil and gas investments were the hottest things going. But many people who invested money in oil and gas did not understand the risks involved, and the vast majority lost their investments when the prices fell and marginal wells became unprofitable.

A high degree of risk exists, particularly in oil exploration. In an effort to reduce that risk, many people invested in oil and gas limited partnerships in known gas and oil fields. Not only did they lose their money on these investments, but they also discovered they were liable for environmental damages caused by the wells.

This kind of an investment is not only very risky but usually very expensive. Again, a glance back at the volatility of the economy over the past several decades gives us insight to current issues and "opportunities." If you plan to invest in oil and gas, risk only a small portion of your assets, and don't let anybody talk you into risking larger amounts.

Commodities Market

(Income 0)(Growth 0-10)(Risk 10+)

Commodities speculation requires a relatively small dollar investment and can bring huge returns, primarily through the use of leverage.

Commodities are appealing, since a $1,000 investment in the commodities market can control $10,000 worth of contracts—or more—for future delivery. But remember: "A fool and his money are soon parted."

Investing in commodities is probably the closest thing to gambling that most Christians ever try. Actually, it is gambling. You can lose everything you own and even more. Commodity prices can move quickly above or below your initial investment, possibly triggering a forced sale that could result in losses exceeding your initial investment.

Collectibles

(Income 0)(Growth 2-10)(Risk 10+)

Antiques, old automobiles, paintings, figurines, and so forth are all collectibles that can be used while you hold them to sell.

One of the most important prerequisites to investing in collectibles is knowledge. You need to know value before investing. Second, you need to put some time and labor into locating the best places to buy and sell. Third, you must have the capital to wait for just the right buyer. Often, novice investors get discouraged and sell out at a loss.

Unless you have a high degree of knowledge in this area, the risk is inordinately high. With most items like antiques, automobiles, figurines, and paintings, you can develop the expertise you need by talking with other people and reading key periodicals. The rate of return on collectibles can easily be 10+, but the risk of loss is just as great.

Precious Gems
(Income 0)(Growth 0-4)(Risk 10+)

Diamonds, opals, rubies, sapphires, and other stones can be purchased for relatively small amounts of money. Then they can be mounted into a ring or pendant and worn while you're waiting for them to appreciate. The pleasure of wearing them may be the highest return you will ever see.

For every person we know who made money in gems, we know a hundred who lost money. It's almost impossible for a novice to know the true value of a gem, even with a "certified" appraisal. Worst of all, it's very difficult to sell gems at a fair price unless you have your own market. The rule here is to stay with what you know or with someone you thoroughly trust.

Limited Partnerships
(Income 0-7)(Growth 0)(Risk 10+)

Limited partnerships are formed to pool investors' money to purchase assets, usually in real properties. The investment is managed by a general partner who has the decision authority for buying and selling.

Since your investment in a limited partnership is no better than the property and the management, the key is to know the general partner's credibility.

A limited partner's liability normally is limited to the amount of money invested. Limited partnerships that carry contingent tax liabilities or require subsequent annual payments or operating loss guarantees should be avoided.

In the past, limited partnerships in properties, such as apartment complexes, office complexes, or shopping centers, were purchased primarily to shelter ordinary income.

But since 1987, most of these benefits have been gradually eliminated, and the tax write-offs can be used only to shelter passive income. For most investors, the risk is too high and the returns too uncertain.

Summary

This basic review of the five major types of investments is by no means an exhaustive review. However, it should provide you with a starting point for an investment strategy after you have developed a surplus in your spending plan.

There are many good materials available on the Web and in most public libraries, including books on investing. Always remember that balance is the key. Be careful about whose advice you take, because so many people are dedicated to the leverage principle.

Evaluate the risk involved with any investment. The higher the promised return, the higher the degree of risk, and the only way you can lower the risk is through your own personal expertise. You have to know what you're doing.

Section 3

ON-THE-JOB INVESTING

One of the best accumulation strategies in the world is a company-sponsored retirement plan. Whether they are called "401(k)" or "403(b)" plans, the names simply refer to the sections of the tax code that authorize company-sponsored retirement plans.

The investments available through a company retirement plan may be the same as those you would choose if you were investing on your own. Depending on the plan and how it is administered, your options can include annuities, mutual funds, company stock, CDs, or any combination of these.

The disadvantage of company retirement plans is that the selection of options you have to choose from is determined by the plan administrator(s). As a result, these options may or may not be the best available to meet your personal goals.

One large advantage of a qualified company retirement plan is that the funds you invest are tax deferred. In other words, taxes are not paid on the money until it is withdrawn. Many companies also offer matching funds, based on a percentage of what you choose to invest.

The sooner you start in a retirement plan, the less risk you will have to assume in order to reach your financial goals.

Your company will provide complete information on the options you have available under any company-sponsored retirement plan. Don't hesitate to ask for help in making the best choices for your specific situation.

Individual Retirement Accounts

The Economic Growth and Tax Relief Act of 2001 has significantly increased the amounts that may be contributed to both traditional IRAs and Roth IRAs. You can contribute to both an IRA and a Roth IRA as long as your combined contributions do not exceed $5,000 per person for the year 2008 ($6,000 if you are over age 50).

Married couples can each have an IRA and contribute up to the limit even if only one of them is employed. The non-working spouse's IRA is referred to as a spousal IRA and is funded by the working spouse. This is true for both traditional and Roth IRAs.

Traditional IRA contributions (within the limits) are tax-deductible. They grow tax-free until withdrawal and are fully taxed when withdrawn.

Roth IRA contributions are not tax-deductible, but they have the advantage of being tax-free when they are withdrawn—including the untaxed gains! Several other relaxed restrictions make Roth IRAs a very wise choice to complement other retirement plans.

Year	IRA and Roth IRA Contribution Limit
2008	$5,000
after 2008	Indexed for inflation

Taxpayers age 50 or over who have earned income can contribute an additional $1,000 over and above the regular contribution limit.

1. **Traditional IRA**—Currently, if an individual or spouse is an active participant in a qualified employer-sponsored retirement plan, the $5,000 IRA deduction* is phased out over certain adjusted gross income levels. The charts below show the limits for various filing status categories. If your adjusted gross income (AGI) falls within the Phase Out range, you are allowed to make a prorated contribution that diminishes as you reach the No Deduction limit.

2008 Traditional IRA AGI Deduction Limits (If Covered by a Retirement Plan at Work)

Filing Status	Full Deduction	Phase Out	No Deduction
Single, head of household	$53,000 or less	$53,000–$63,000	$63,000 or more
Married filing jointly	$85,000 or less	$85,000–$105,000	$105,000 or more
Married filing separately	Less than $10,000	$10,000 or more	

Traditional IRA AGI Deduction Limits (If NOT Covered by a Retirement Plan at Work)

Filing Status	Full Deduction	Phase-Out	No Deduction
Single, head of household	No Limit	No Limit	No Limit
Married filing jointly (spouse not covered)	No Limit	No Limit	No Limit
Married filing jointly (spouse covered)	$159,000 or less	$159,001–$169,000	$169,001 or more
Married filing separately (spouse covered)	Less than $10,000	$10,000 or more	

2. **Roth IRA**—The contribution* limit of $5,000 for 2008 is reduced for incomes within the Phase Out range shown below.

Roth IRA Income Limits

Filing Status	Full Contribution	Contribution Phase Out	No Contributions
Single filers	$101,000	$101,001–$116,000	$114,000 or more
Joint filers	$159,000	$159,001–$169,000	$169,001

Qualified distributions from Roth IRAs are not taxed:

- if such distributions are made at least five years after the contribution was made and are taken after age 59½,
- in the event of death,
- in the event of disability,
- when used for buying a first home, or
- when used to pay higher education expenses.

Roth IRAs also have the advantage of not requiring withdrawals at any age as opposed to traditional IRAs that require them (along with paying the resulting taxes) at age 70½.

In addition, the tax advantages of a Roth account make it a great estate asset. An inherited Roth can give your beneficiary substantially more value than an equal amount of normal after-tax dollars.

* **DEDUCTION vs. CONTRIBUTION** – The **traditional IRA** uses the term "deduction" in its income-based limits rather than "contribution" because the two terms are definitely different. If your income exceeds the amount that allows you to deduct a traditional IRA contribution from current taxable income, you can still make a nondeductible contribution to your traditional IRA. At some income levels, part of your contribution is deductible and part is not. Any time you make a nondeductible contribution to a traditional IRA, you need to report it on Form 8606. When you begin taking distributions, the nondeductible contributions you made will escape taxation; their earnings, however, will be taxed—as will all deductible contributions and their earnings.

The **Roth IRA** chart uses the term "contribution" rather than "deduction" because no Roth contributions are deductible. If you earn more than $101,000 as a single filer, you can make a reduced contribution; earning more than $114,000 means you cannot make any Roth contribution for the year.

3. **Coverdell Education Savings Accounts**—Parents can establish education IRAs for each child and make annual nondeductible contributions of up to $2,000 to each. This privilege is above and beyond your ability to make contributions to traditional and Roth IRAs. Earnings on education IRA funds accumulate tax-free, and tax-free withdrawals can be made to pay for elementary school, secondary school, undergraduate or graduate education expenses. This includes expenses for tuition, books, room and board, and purchase of a computer system, educational software, and Internet access.

   The ability to make contributions is phased out between AGI of $190,000 and $220,000 for joint filers and between $95,000 and $110,000 for single taxpayers. Subject to the preceding limitations, grandparents and others can establish education IRAs to benefit grandchildren and other designated individuals.

Section 4

INVESTMENT COUNSELING

Have you ever wondered where you can go to get good investment advice? There is no "right" answer to the question. In large part, it depends on your age, income, and temperament. Options include everything from an inexpensive magazine or newsletter to very expensive professional counsel.

Before seeking investment advice, you first need to make sure you are prepared to invest. Living within your means is the first level, or foundation, of investing. You must be able to manage the money you earn in order to create a surplus to invest. This means creating a spending plan.

Everyone needs a spending plan, even those with higher incomes. It is impossible to be a good steward of what God has entrusted to you if you don't manage it well. Obviously, those with less income also need spending plans or they will never develop a surplus that can be multiplied.

HELP *Counseling for Novice Investors*

Once you have a workable spending plan and develop a surplus to invest, learn as much as you can before taking any risks.

Usually, the counselors or advisors available to low-budget investors are commissioned salespeople who make their living by selling products like insurance, mutual funds, and annuities. The entry-level investor simply doesn't have enough money to buy the services of a professional investment advisor.

Therefore, novice investors have three basic options:

1. Do their own investing and pay the price of learning as they go.
2. Take the advice of salespeople and hope they sell a quality product.
3. Seek inexpensive written materials they can rely on for guidance.

Fortunately, many good materials are available to educate nonprofessional investors.

Usually, first-time investors subscribe to too many resources. This often results in confusion and frustration as one publication contradicts another. The key is to select resources that don't push a particular agenda, such as precious metals, insurance, mutual funds, etc.

Newsletters and Web sites can be a good source of basic advice. Low-budget or first-time investors should subscribe to newsletters written specifically for them. It's crucial to verify the track record of the managing editor, since usually that person is the primary advice giver.Look for a newsletter that takes the first-time investor through each phase of learning, including specific advice about what investments to use at each level of income.

In summary, potential investors should keep one important point in mind: "Let the buyer beware." Be prudent when selecting investments and always seek wise counsel. Above all, pray about every investment decision you make.

Commissioned Salespeople

The next step up in investment advice involves people who sell a product (or products) and generate commissions (as opposed to charging a fee).

This type of investment counselor varies broadly. Some are very qualified to give good, objective counsel and also earn commissions in the process. Others are novices or incompetents. They sell only what they've been taught to sell and offer little or no balance in their advice.

One way to find a good advisor is to require several references from others with whom the salesperson has worked. Check with at least three of the advisor's clients to verify his or her track record.

It is important that these clients have been dealing with the advisor for at least three years. If the advisor won't provide such references, look elsewhere for advice.

Some commissioned salespeople try to talk you into buying from them because they're Christians (or church members). And they try to make you feel guilty if you don't. Avoid them with all diligence. If an agent's products and track record will not stand by themselves, stay away. Otherwise, you'll probably lose your money as well as your friend.

Also avoid the "doom-and-gloomers," who talk about coming economic disasters and then try to sell you "collapse proof" investments, such as gold and silver.

Fee-Plus-Commission Advisors

In addition to advisors who make their incomes exclusively from commission sales, there are a growing number of investment advisors who will work either way—fees or commission sales, or both.

Usually, these advisors will initially provide counsel for a fixed fee per hour. Then, if you elect to buy products from them, they'll reduce the fee by the commissions they receive.

Prudent investors recognize that advisors usually exercise significant influence over their clients. In many instances, this means investors end up buying what the advisors recommend, which are usually the products they sell.

The question then becomes whether the fee-plus-commission is really a ploy to get clients to buy from them while thinking they are receiving objective advice. That totally depends on the character of the advisor—something you will need to discern for yourself.

A simple comparison of the value and prices of the products suggested will tell you whether the advisor is totally objective. If the investment products he or she offers are as good as those offered through other agents, then why not buy from your advisor? But if what he or she offers is inferior or higher priced, avoid the advice as well as the product.

Fee-Only Investment Advisors

A fee-only advisor is exactly what the name implies. He or she charges a fee but does not sell any products or accept commissions—usually. We say "usually" because some advisors who advertised themselves as fee-only planners accept commissions, known as "finder's fees," from product companies.

Because they generate their income from fees, you can expect fee-only advisors to be expensive. Most cater to the upper-income investor and often require a minimum level of net worth for the clients they advise. The fees can range from several hundred dollars for a one-time evaluation to several thousand a year for continuing clients.

In general, I have not found fee-only advisors to be any more accurate in their advice than a well-seasoned fee-plus-commission advisor, although there are exceptions. The one area in which fee-only planners usually excel is in designing long-term investment strategies for their clients.

Since follow-up is so essential, they usually do a good job of getting their clients to implement their plans. After all, if you're paying someone $10,000 a year to advise you, usually you'll do what they say.

Fee-Only Versus Commission

No matter which type of advisor you're considering, check out his or her track record carefully. It doesn't matter whether you pay your advisor by way of a fee or a commission. What matters is, will your advisor make more money for you than he or she will cost you?

A commissioned salesperson who makes 12 percent for clients after all commissions, administrative charges, and market fluctuations are taken into account is still better than a fee-only planner who makes 6 percent for clients after all costs.

Remember to ask for at least three local people you can talk to about your advisor's track record. If you can't get these references, look for another advisor.

Christian or Non-Christian Advisors?

Psalm 1:1-2 says, *"How blessed is the man who does not walk in the counsel of the wicked, nor stand in the path of sinners, nor sit in the seat of scoffers! But his delight is in the law of the Lord, and in His law he meditates day and night."*

There's a clear implication here that our primary source of counsel should be from those who know the Lord. Does this imply that we should never take counsel from an unbeliever? I don't think so. I believe the implication is not to rely on secular counsel as our daily source of wisdom. All counsel should be weighed against God's wisdom and discarded if it fails the test. That includes Christian and non-Christian counsel.

Where Do You Find a Good Investment Advisor?

There is no perfect formula for finding a good investment advisor, but you can make your search easier.

1. Contact *KingdomAdvisors.org* for a recommended Christian financial professional. Kingdom Advisors, led by Ron Blue and founded by Larry Burkett, is devoted to equipping Christian financial advisors to apply biblical wisdom to their advice and counsel.

2. Ask in your church and Bible studies for references. Ask people who give you references if they have made money with the advisors they are recommending. Look

for an advisor with at least five years of experience (10 if possible). Anyone can guess right one time, but that doesn't establish a track record. If an advisor hasn't ridden out at least one major recession in his or her field, in my opinion that advisor is still a novice.

3. Check an advisor's credentials with the National Association of Securities Dealers if he or she is a registered broker. If this advisor has ever had his or her license suspended or revoked, be very cautious.
4. Check with several local accountants who do tax returns for people you know. Often they see the bad as well as the good side of an advisor. Although most accountants will hesitate to give a bad report on a bad advisor, most will not hesitate to give a good report on a good advisor.
5. Check to see if an advisor has earned professional designations such as CFP® (Certified Financial Planner), CLU (Chartered Life Underwriter) and ChFC (Chartered Financial Consultant). These designations won't guarantee that a particular advisor is best for you, but at the very least they show that the advisor has completed a disciplined course of study.

Discount Brokers

During the last decade or so, many discount brokerage firms have been started. These firms will place investment orders for very low commissions. This trend is certain to grow as banks expand further into the investment area.

Once you have a level of expertise that allows you the freedom to make your own investment decisions, the use of a discount broker can save you money when trading in individual stocks, bonds, mutual funds, etc.

Section 5

IMPORTANT GOALS FOR INVESTORS

Establish a "Safety Net" of Cash and Insurance

One of the most important goals to consider when you invest money is the creation of a "safety net" to provide for your family in the event of a catastrophe.

This includes a cash reserve large enough to cover three to six months of living expenses. Of course, this reserve should be in a highly liquid account. In other words, you should be able to withdraw this money easily when you need it.

Another part of your safety net should be life insurance to provide income for your family in the event of your death. Having insurance and a cash reserve reduces the likelihood of needing to sell a long-term investment prematurely or at an inopportune time.

Get Started Early

When you start investing early in life, you spread the task of accumulating funds over a longer period of time. For example, suppose you want to accumulate $300,000 by age 65. Assuming a 10 percent compounded rate of return, you'll need to put away $47 per month if you begin investing at age 25.

If you begin at 35, you'll need to put away $133 per month. At age 45, the monthly amount is $395. And at 55, it jumps to $1,464.

Investing early in life depends on how much surplus a young couple or single person has. The amount of surplus depends on lifestyle.

Unfortunately, too many young people jump head over heels into debt by purchasing homes that are far too expensive for their income. Then, they add to their debt load by purchasing high-priced adult toys like luxury cars, boats, and swimming pools. As a consequence, they can't pay off their mortgage early, and they have little or no money to set aside in a company retirement account.

In Section 1 we noted that early repayment of your house mortgage should be your first investment priority. We made an exception for a company retirement account with matching funds of at least 25 percent.

Living beyond your means will make it impossible to pay off your mortgage early or make any other meaningful investment. Accepting a less expensive house can make all the difference, allowing you to pay it off early and then have plenty of money available to invest.

How quickly can you retire a mortgage? Let's use the example of a $100,000 mortgage at 10 percent for 30 years. By paying only $100 extra per month toward the principal you can retire that mortgage about 11 years early and save $113,000 in interest!

Give Your Money the Freedom to Grow

The more constraints you place on your investment program, the more likely it is that your investment results will fail to meet your expectations. Earning too little on your investments is one of the greatest obstacles to investment success, along with starting too late. It is important that you keep pace with inflation.

It's not enough just to preserve what you have now. You need to make your money grow just to stay even with the rising cost of living. Let's consider the effect of inflation over the last 82 years. The average rate of inflation over 82 years (1926 to 2007) has been 3.0 percent annually. What you could buy for $1 in 1926 now costs $12.00 according to the Ibbotson.®

Let's apply this to retirement savings. If you assume (could be dangerous) that future inflation will mirror the past, you know that your monthly income will need to grow every year in order to keep the same purchasing power. If you think you can retire comfortably on $4,000 per month beginning now, in 30 years your $4,000 per month would need to be $9,827 per month. Sobering, isn't it?

This is not to suggest that you pour all your money into a high-risk investment with a high rate of return. But on the other hand, you wouldn't want to invest all your money in T-bills. The "Rule of 72" is a useful tool in demonstrating the importance of your investment return. Simply divide 72 by the rate of return, and the quotient will tell you how many years it will take for your investment value to double.

Let's assume your rate of return is 6 percent. If you divide 72 by 6, the quotient is 12. So, it will take 12 years for your investment value to double with a 6 percent rate of return. Now, let's assume your rate of return is 12 percent. If you divide 72 by 12, the quotient is 6. By doubling your rate of return, you cut in half the years required to double your investment.

It should be obvious at this point that, over the long haul, bank savings accounts and CDs are not the best place for all of your investment dollars. And the portion of your money that you do invest at the bank doesn't necessarily have to go into a CD or savings account. Investigate money market accounts, and compare various bank rates because they can vary considerably from product to product and institution to institution.

Use Strategies That Provide Safety and Return

Using some higher-risk investments to help counter the effects of inflation does not mean throwing caution to the wind. The risks associated with these investments can be reduced enough to satisfy most investors. The solution is to use risk-minimizing strategies. Several are listed below.

Diversification

Discussed in Section 1 (Key #6).

Professional Management

One way to avoid investment errors is to have your investment portfolio managed by a qualified professional, which can be a costly proposition. But even if you have just a small amount of money to invest, there's still a way to get the benefits of professional management. That's what mutual funds provide.

Since mutual funds vary tremendously in performance—even within their own category—shop carefully to select funds that consistently perform at or near the top of their category. Financial magazines regularly list these. Online brokerages typically have powerful screening tools that will help you find the best funds.

Investing for the Long Term

Discussed in Section 1 (Key #7).

Asset Allocation

This means dividing your investment dollars into percentages, which you then put into different groups of investments. You might want to use the five tiers described in Section 2.

For example, you might put 20 percent of your money into Tier I, which is Secure Income. You might put 40 percent into Tier II (Long-Term Income), 30 percent into Tier III (Growth Investments), 10 percent into Tier IV (Speculative Growth Investments), and nothing into Tier V (High Risk Investments).

The younger you are, the more likely you will want to have higher percentages in Tier III and IV investments, but the percentage you put into each tier will depend on your individual goals, needs, philosophy, and risk tolerance.

Dollar Cost Averaging

Consistency is important if you want the best return on your investment dollar. Dollar cost averaging means that you regularly add a certain amount into a particular investment.

For example, you might want to set aside $50 per month to invest in a mutual fund or buy shares of stock in a particular company. Each investment you made in the mutual fund would buy a certain number of shares in the fund, depending on what the share price was at that particular time. Both the share prices for stocks and mutual funds would fluctuate.

The following example shows the benefits of dollar cost averaging in a market in which share prices are declining. In this example, the regular investment is $200, which is made once per quarter.

Quarter Amount	Quarterly Price	Share Purchased	Shares
1st Qtr.	$200	$25.00	8
2nd Qtr.	$200	$20.00	10
3rd Qtr.	$200	$12.50	16
4th Qtr.	$200	$10.00	20
Total:	$800	$67.50	54

Average quarterly price per share ($67.50 ÷ 4) = $16.88
Price per share with dollar cost averaging ($800 ÷ 54) = $14.81

Puzzling? This lower cost per share with dollar cost averaging occurs because you get more shares for your $200 when the price is lower.

Perhaps the bigger question is: Would you want to keep buying this stock? Maybe. Some pros would say yes and others would say no, depending on the situation, but that's one of the reasons a mutual fund provides more comfort. It's less volatile, and dollar cost averaging works just the same.

Build from Quality

Investing is like building a reserve for the future. Be sure the products you select are quality products.

Your Response

Action Steps

Celebration Plan

CHAPTER 3

WRAPPING IT UP WITH HOPE

Insurance and investing can be intimidating subjects because of their complexity, but both are intended to be your friends. They exist to improve the quality of your life and to help you manage the resources God has entrusted to your care.

Rather than let a lack of knowledge paralyze you or fill you with fear, recognize it as a temporary condition that can be cured. God encourages us to look to Him for wisdom and to ask with confidence: *"But if any of you lacks wisdom, let him ask of God, who gives to all generously and without reproach, and it will be given to him"* (James 1:5).

God's direction is not likely to come in a heavenly billboard listing policy specifications and stocks to buy, but don't underestimate its value.

- He has gifted others within His body with detailed insurance and investment knowledge.
- He has directed you to seek their counsel.
- He has given you a mind with which to make decisions.

- His Spirit illuminates your mind regarding His purposes for you.
- He wants you to trust Him (attitude) and be a good steward (action).

It is comforting to know that Jesus, through direct experience, can identify with our weaknesses. *"For we do not have a high priest who cannot sympathize with our weaknesses, but One who has been tempted in all things as we are, yet without sin"* (Hebrews 4:15).

It's even more comforting to know that after overcoming weaknesses and temptations, He didn't wash His hands of us and declare us unfit for companionship. Instead, He valued us enough to give His life in exchange for ours and then to give us His never-ending presence in the form of His Spirit to reside inside of us.

How should we respond? *"Therefore let us draw near with confidence to the throne of grace, so that we may receive mercy and find grace to help in time of need"* (Hebrews 4:16).

How great is that! God is waiting to meet your requests with mercy and grace, illuminating your path as you grow in trust and obedience.

Your Response

Action Steps

Celebration Plan

APPENDIX 1

INTRODUCTION TO CHRIST

As important as our financial welfare is, it is not our highest priority. The single most important need of every person everywhere is to know God and experience the gift of His forgiveness and peace.

These five biblical truths will show you God's open door through a personal relationship with Jesus Christ.

1. **God loves you and wants you to know Him and experience a meaningful life.**

   God created people in His own image, and He desires a close relationship with each of us. *"For God so loved the world, that He gave His only begotten Son, that whoever believes in Him shall not perish, but have eternal life"* (John 3:16). *"I [Jesus] came that they might have life, and have it abundantly"* (John 10:10).

   God the Father loved you so much that He gave His only Son, Jesus Christ, to die for you.

2. Unfortunately, we are separated from God.

Because God is holy and perfect, no sin can abide in His presence. Every person has sinned, and the consequence of sin is separation from God. *"All have sinned and fall short of the glory of God"* (Romans 3:23). *"Your sins have cut you off from God"* (Isaiah 59:2, TLB).

3. God's only provision to bridge this gap is Jesus Christ.

Jesus Christ died on the cross to pay the penalty for our sin, bridging the gap between God and us. Jesus said, *"I am the way, and the truth, and the life; no one comes to the Father but through Me"* (John 14:6). *"God demonstrates His own love towards us, in that while we were yet sinners, Christ died for us"* (Romans 5:8).

4. This relationship is a gift from God.

Our efforts can never achieve the perfection God requires. The only solution was to provide it to us as a gift.

When Jesus bore our sins on the cross, paying our penalty forever, He exchanged His righteousness for our guilt. By faith, we receive the gift we could never deserve.

Is that fair? Of course not! God's love exceeds His justice, resulting in mercy and grace toward us.

"It is by grace you have been saved, through faith—and this is not from yourselves, it is the gift of God—not by works, so that no one can boast" (Ephesians 2:8-9, NIV).

5. **We must each receive Jesus Christ individually.**

   Someone has said that God has no grandchildren. Each of us is responsible before God for our own sin. We can continue to bear the responsibility and pay the consequences or we can receive the gift of Jesus' righteousness, enabling God to declare us "Not guilty!"

If you desire to know the Lord and are not certain whether you have this relationship, we encourage you to receive Christ right now. Pray a prayer similar to this suggested one:

> ***"God, I need You. I invite Jesus to come into my life as my Savior and Lord and to make me the person You want me to be. Thank You for forgiving my sins and for giving me the gift of eternal life."***

You may be successful in avoiding financial quicksand—and we pray you will be—but without a relationship with Christ, it won't have lasting value. Eternal perspective begins with Him.

If you ask Christ into your life, please tell some people you know who are also following Christ. They will encourage you and help you get involved in a Bible-teaching church where you can grow spiritually. And please let us know as well. We would love to help in any way we can.

APPENDIX 2

GOD'S OWNERSHIP & FINANCIAL FAITHFULNESS

How we view God determines how we live. Viewing Him as Savior is a good beginning, but growth comes when we view Him as Lord.

After losing his children and all his possessions, Job continued to worship God because he knew God was the Lord of those possessions and retained the ultimate rights over them. Realizing that God owed him nothing and he owed God everything enabled him to submit to God's authority and find contentment.

Moses walked away from his earthly inheritance, regarding *"disgrace for the sake of Christ as of greater value than the treasures of Egypt"* because he had his eye on God's reward (Hebrews 11:26, NIV).

Our willingness, like theirs, to give up a lesser value for a greater one, requires recognizing what most of the world does not: God is not only the Creator and Owner of all but also the ultimate definer of value. Those responsibilities belong to Him. He has retained them because He alone is capable of handling them.

Most of the frustration we experience in handling money comes when we take God's responsibilities on our own shoulders. Successful money management requires us to understand three aspects of God's Lordship—three roles for which He retains responsibility.

1. GOD OWNS IT ALL.

God owns all our possessions. *"To the Lord your God belong . . . the earth and everything in it"* (Deuteronomy 10:14, NIV). *"The earth is the Lord's, and all it contains"* (Psalm 24:1).

Leviticus 25:23 identifies Him as the owner of all the land: *"The land . . . shall not be sold permanently, for the land is Mine."* Haggai 2:8 says that He owns the precious metals: *"'The silver is Mine and the gold is Mine,' declares the Lord of hosts."*

Even our body—the one thing for which we would tend to claim total ownership—is not our own. *"Or do you not know that your body is a temple of the Holy Spirit who is in you, whom you have from God, and that you are not your own?"* (1 Corinthians 6:19).

The Lord created all things, and He never transferred the ownership of His creation to people. In Colossians 1:17 we are told that, *"In Him all things hold together."* At this very moment the Lord holds everything together by His power. As we will see throughout this study, recognizing God's ownership is crucial in allowing Jesus Christ to become the Lord of our money and possessions.

• Yielding Our Ownership to His Lordship

If we are to be genuine followers of Christ, we must transfer ownership of our possessions to Him. *"None of you can be My disciple who does not give up all his own possessions"* (Luke 14:33). Sometimes He tests us by asking us to give up the very possessions that are most important to us.

The most vivid example of this in Scripture is when God instructed Abraham, *"Take now your son, your only son, whom you love, Isaac . . . and offer him there as a burnt offering"* (Genesis 22:2). When Abraham obeyed, demonstrating his willingness to give up his most valuable possession, God responded, *"Do not lay a hand on the boy . . . now I know that you fear God, because you have not withheld from Me your son"* (Genesis 22:12, NIV).

When we acknowledge God's ownership, every spending decision becomes a spiritual decision. No longer do we ask, "Lord, what do You want me to do with my money?" It becomes, "Lord, what do You want me to do with Your money?" When we have this attitude and handle His money according to His wishes, spending and saving decisions become as spiritual as giving decisions.

• Recognizing God's Ownership

Our culture—the media, even the law—says that what you possess, you own. Acknowledging God's ownership requires a transformation of thinking, and this can be difficult. Many people say that God owns it all while they cling desperately to possessions that they think define them.

Here are a number of practical suggestions to help us recognize God's ownership.

- For the next 30 days, meditate on 1 Chronicles 29:11-12 when you first awake and just before going to sleep.
- For the next 30 days, ask God to make you aware of His ownership and help you to be thankful for it.
- Establish the habit of acknowledging God's ownership every time you buy something.

Recognizing God's ownership is important in learning contentment. When you believe you own something, you are more vulnerable to its circumstances. If it suffers loss or damage, your attitude can swing quickly from happy to discontented.

Recognizing it as God's loss doesn't make it irrelevant, but it does change your perspective. Now you can focus on how He will use this incident in causing *"all things to work together for good to those who love God, to those who are called according to His purpose"* (Romans 8:28).

2. GOD CONTROLS IT ALL.

Besides being Creator and Owner, God is ultimately in control of every event that occurs upon the earth. *"We adore you as being in control of everything"* (1 Chronicles 29:11, TLB). *"Whatever the Lord pleases, He does, in heaven and in earth"* (Psalm 135:6). And in the book of Daniel, King Nebuchadnezzar stated: *"I praised the Most High; I honored and glorified him who lives forever. . . . He does as he pleases with the powers of heaven and the peoples of the earth. No one can hold back his hand or say to him: 'What have you done?'"* (Daniel 4:34-35, NIV).

God is also in control of difficult events. *"I am the Lord, and there is no other, the One forming light and creating darkness, causing well-being and creating calamity; I am the Lord who does all these"* (Isaiah 45:6-7).

It is important for us to realize that our heavenly Father uses even seemingly devastating circumstances for ultimate good in the lives of the godly. *"We know that God causes all things to work together for good to those who love God, to those who are called according to His purpose"* (Romans 8:28). God allows difficult circumstances for three reasons.

- **He accomplishes His intentions.**

This is illustrated in the life of Joseph, who was sold into slavery as a teenager by his jealous brothers. Joseph later said to his brothers: *"Do not be distressed and do not be angry with yourselves for selling me here, because it was to save lives that God sent me ahead of you. . . . It was not you who sent me here, but God. . . . You intended to harm me, but God intended it for good to accomplish what is now being done, the saving of many lives"* (Genesis 45:5, 8; 50:20, NIV).

- **He develops our character.**

Godly character, something that is precious in His sight, is often developed during trying times. *"We also rejoice in our sufferings, because we know that suffering produces perseverance; perseverance, character"* (Romans 5:3-4, NIV).

- **He disciplines His children.**

"Those whom the Lord loves He disciplines. . . . He disciplines us for our good, so that we may share His holiness. All discipline for the moment seems not to be joyful, but sorrowful; yet to those who have been trained by it, afterwards it yields the peaceful fruit of righteousness" (Hebrews 12:6,10-11).

When we are disobedient, we can expect our loving Lord to discipline us, often through difficult circumstances. His purpose is to encourage us to abandon our sin and to "share His holiness."

You can be at peace knowing that your loving heavenly Father is in control of every situation you will ever face. He will use every one of them for a good purpose.

3. GOD PROVIDES IT ALL.

God promises to provide our needs. *"But seek first His kingdom and His righteousness, and all these things [food and clothing] will be added to you"* (Matthew 6:33).

The same God who fed manna to the children of Israel during their 40 years of wandering in the wilderness and who fed 5,000 with only five loaves and two fish has promised to provide our needs. This is the same God who told Elijah, *"I have commanded the ravens to provide for you there. . . . The ravens brought him bread and meat in the morning and bread and meat in the evening"* (1 Kings 17:4, 6).

God—Both Predictable and Unpredictable

God is totally predictable in His faithfulness to provide for our needs. What we cannot predict is how He will provide. He uses various and often surprising means—an increase in income or a gift. He may provide an opportunity to stretch limited resources through money-saving purchases. Regardless of how He chooses to provide for our needs, He is completely reliable.

Our culture believes that God plays no part in financial matters; they assume that His invisibility means He is uninvolved. They try to shoulder responsibilities that God never intended for them—burdens of ownership, control, and provision that only He can carry.

Jesus said, *"Come to Me, all who are weary and heavy-laden, and I will give you rest. Take My yoke upon you. . . . For My yoke is easy, and My burden is light"* (Matthew 11:28-30). This is the only way we can rest and enjoy the peace of God.

When we trust God to do His part in our finances, we can focus on doing our part: being financially faithful with every resource He has given us.

Defining Financial Faithfulness

Faithfully living by God's financial principles doesn't necessarily mean having a pile of money in the bank, but it does bring an end to overdue bills and their related stress. And that's not the most important part; that's just relief from symptoms.

Consider some of the big-picture benefits:

- Assurance that God is in control of our circumstances
- Absolute faith in His promise to meet all of our needs
- A clear conscience before God
- A clear conscience with others

This is not to say that we will live on financial autopilot with no more challenges for the rest of our lives. God promises no such thing. In fact, without challenges our faith has no opportunity to be perfected or even to grow; without challenges it isn't active or visible. But peace in the midst of challenges is a miraculous quality of life, and that's what God promises when we learn to trust and follow Him fully.

With God in control, we have nothing to fear. He is the Master of the universe. His wisdom is superior to ours in every way, and no situation is too complex or hopeless for Him to solve.

God has even provided a solution for our ongoing frailties and failings. As part of His great redemption, He offers continuing forgiveness and cleansing from all unrighteousness (1 John 1:9). We make mistakes—sometimes willfully violating His plan for us—but He welcomes our confession and honors it by restoring our fellowship and renewing our guidance.

Once we begin to experience the rewards of financial faithfulness, we never want to be without them. Our deepening trust in *God's* faithfulness intensifies our desire to stay within His will, resulting in perfect peace.

Many people have inherited or achieved financial independence: a level of wealth that requires no further work or income. But apart from Christ, they don't have freedom from anxiety; they have merely replaced one set of worries with another. They often fear:

- Loss of what they have accumulated
- Loss of meaningful relationships—fearing that others only care about what they have rather than who they are
- Loss of safety as their wealth makes them a target for theft or kidnapping
- Loss of grace from others, who jealously hold them to a higher standard because of their wealth

Being financially free, on the other hand, includes freedom from these fears as well as from the oppression of envy, covetousness, and greed.

Financial faithfulness is transformation—a process that requires God's power and our participation. It is synonymous with our definition of true financial faithfulness in the *Crown Money Map™*:

1. Knowing that God owns it all.
2. Finding contentment with what He provides.
3. Being free to be all He made you to be.

This is the big picture, the framework within which wealth and material possessions take their rightful place—not as ends but as means—in God's hands.

Steps to Cultivate Financial Faithfulness

Now it is time to outline the path. Since we're talking about transformation, you'll notice that some of our steps go well beyond mere money-management techniques.

1. TRANSFER OWNERSHIP.

Transferring ownership of every possession to God means acknowledging that He already owns them and that we will begin treating them accordingly. This includes more than just material possessions; it includes money, time, family, education, even earning potential for the future. This is essential to experience the Spirit-filled life in the area of finances (see Psalm 8:4-6).

There is no substitute for this step. If we believe we are the owners of even a single possession, then the events affecting that possession are going to affect our attitudes. God will not input His perfect will into our lives unless we first surrender our wills to Him.

However, if we make a total transfer of everything to God, He will demonstrate His ability. It is important to understand and accept God's conditions for His control (see Deuteronomy 5:32-33). God will keep His promise to provide our every need according to His perfect plan.

It is easy to say we will make a total transfer of everything to God, but it's not so easy to do. Our desire for control and our habit of self-management cause difficulty in consistently seeking God's will in the area of material things. But without a deep conviction that He is in control, we can never experience true financial faithfulness.

What a great relief it is to turn our burdens over to Him. Then, if something happens to the car, we can say, "Father, I gave this car to You; I've maintained it to the best of my ability, but I don't own it. It belongs to You, so do with it whatever You like." Then look for the blessing God has in store as a result of this attitude.

2. BECOME DEBT FREE.

God wants us to be free to serve Him without restriction. *"You were bought with a price; do not become slaves of men"* (1 Corinthians 7:23). *"The rich rules over the poor, and the borrower becomes the lender's slave"* (Proverbs 22:7).

Read *Debt and Bankruptcy*, another book in the *MoneyLife™ Basics Series*, for further information on this, including definitions and steps for getting out of debt. For most, this will involve sacrifice—at least initially—but the payoff is well worth it.

3. GIVE REGULARLY AND GENEROUSLY.

Every follower of Christ should establish tithing (10 percent of income) as a beginning point of giving and as a testimony to God's ownership. We can't say we have given total ownership to God if our actions don't back the claim.

It is through sharing that we bring His power in finances into focus. In every case, God wants us to give the first part to Him, but He also wants us to pay our creditors. This requires establishing a plan, and it will probably mean making sacrifices of wants and desires until all obligations are current.

We cannot sacrifice God's part—that is not our prerogative as faithful, obedient followers of Christ. Malachi 3:8-9 has strong words for those who "rob God." But then verses 10-12 describe His great blessing for those who tithe fully.

God, as the first giver, wants us to be like Him, and His economy rewards our generosity. *"Now this I say, he who sows sparingly will also reap sparingly, and he who sows bountifully will also reap bountifully"* (2 Corinthians 9:6).

Steps two and three combine to form an important conclusion. If, while en route to financial faithfulness, sacrifice becomes necessary—and it almost always does—our sacrifice must not come from God's or our creditor's share. We must choose areas within our other discretionary expenses to sacrifice. Consider it an opportunity to exercise faith in God's reward for our obedience.

4. ACCEPT GOD'S PROVISION.

To obtain financial peace, recognize and accept that God's provision is used to direct each of our lives. Often Christians lose sight of the fact that God's will can be accomplished through a withholding of funds; we think that He can direct us only by an abundance of money. But God does not choose for everyone to live in great abundance. This does not imply poverty, but it may mean that God wants us to be more responsive to His day-by-day control.

Followers of Christ must learn to live on what God provides and not give in to a driving desire for wealth or the pressure brought on by comparison with others. This necessitates planning our lifestyle within the provision God has supplied. When we are content to do this, God will always help us find a way.

5. KEEP A CLEAR CONSCIENCE.

Living with integrity means dealing with the past as well as the present. Part of becoming financially faithful requires gaining a clear conscience regarding past business practices and personal dealings. Sometimes, in addition to a changed attitude, our transformation means making restitution for situations where we have wronged someone.

Tim's story is a good example. Before he accepted Christ, he cheated someone out of some money. God convicted him about this and indicated that he should go and make restitution. He contacted the person, confessed what had been done, and offered to make it right. The person refused to forgive and also refused to take any money.

Tim's ego and pride were hurt until he realized that he had been both obedient and successful. His confession was not primarily for the offended person but for his own relationship with God. He had done exactly what God had asked, and God had forgiven him. Nothing further was required.

6. PUT OTHERS FIRST.

This does not imply being a door mat; it simply means that we shouldn't profit at the unfair expense of someone else. As is often the case, attitude is all-important.

7. MANAGE TIME PRIORITIES.

A workaholic might gain wealth at the expense of the family's relational needs, but wealth alone is no indicator of financial faithfulness. And wealth gained with wrong priorities is likely to vanish. *"Do not weary yourself to gain wealth, cease from your consideration of it. When you set your eyes on it, it is gone. For wealth certainly makes itself wings like an eagle that flies toward the heavens"* (Proverbs 23:4-5). Even if it doesn't vanish, it can't deliver the satisfaction it promises. Don't be deceived by overcommitment to business or the pursuit of wealth.

God's priorities for us are very clear.

Priority number one is to develop our relationship with Jesus Christ.

Priority number two is our family. This includes teaching them God's Word. And that requires quality time, something that can't exist without a sufficient quantity from which to flow.

Develop the habit of a regular time to study God's Word for yourself as well as a family time that acknowledges your commitment to each other and to God.

Turn off the television, have the children do their homework early, and begin to study the Bible together. Pray for each other and for those in need. Help your children become intercessors who can pray for others and expect God to answer.

Priority number three is your work, which God intends to be an opportunity for ministry and personal development in addition to providing an income.

Priority number four is church activities and other ministry. This does not imply that it is unimportant or can be neglected, but it keeps us from using church as an excuse to let higher priorities slide. If we observe priority number one, we will not neglect our church.

8. AVOID OVER-INDULGENCE.

Jesus said, *"If anyone wishes to come after Me, he must deny himself, and take up his cross daily and follow Me"* (Luke 9:23). Once again, this is about priorities. Who wins the contest between God's claim on your life and your own pursuit of pleasure?

In Philippians 3:18-19, Paul says that many live as the enemies of the cross of Christ, and he describes them by saying, *"Their destiny is destruction, their god is their stomach, and their glory is in their shame"* (NIV).

That sounds alarmingly like much of our culture, and it takes great effort to avoid being swept along with the current.

9. GET CHRISTIAN COUNSEL.

"Without consultation, plans are frustrated, but with many counselors they succeed" (Proverbs 15:22). God admonishes us to seek counsel and not to rely solely on our own resources. People are often frustrated in financial planning because they lack the necessary knowledge. A common but tragic response is to give up. Within the body of Christ, God has supplied those who have the ability to help in the area of finances. Seek Christian counselors.

To read more on what God says about handling money, go to Crown.org and click "Bible Tools."

OTHER MoneyLife™ BASICS SERIES BOOKS

Pocket-Sized Help and Hope

ISBN 978-1-56427-251-5

◀ Understand the pitfalls of debt, the ins and outs of bankruptcy, and the dangers of gambling

ISBN 978-1-56427-252-2

▲ Create a successful spending plan, and plan for major purchases like homes and automobiles

ISBN 978-1-56427-254-6

◀ Apply biblical wisdom related to making money in work and business

To learn more about the entire series, contact your local book retailer or go to Crown.org.